"In reading about the lives of Dub and Doris Jackson, you will be blessed and challenged to learn how God took two people who were totally dedicated to Him and used them down through the years in ways they never dreamed.

"From their missionary days, primarily in Japan, they fanned out around the world with missions that proclaimed the gospel in country after country.

"Perhaps God will use their story to challenge you to follow their example by going forth to proclaim the gospel around the world."

— Billy Graham —

"Dub Jackson's determination to take our great God and Savior's Great Commission seriously has produced untold numbers of believers for His kingdom. His unswerving belief in impacting a country for Christ in equal partnership with nationals will be an inspiration to every leader."

— Bill Bright —
Founder, Campus Crusade for Christ

"This book is about the incredible moving of God in the lives of real people, just like you and me. It is about the sacrifice that has brought now hundreds of thousands of people on partnership missions and millions into the kingdom of God through their witness. This book throbs with life and whets the appetite for more. Every born-again Christian ought to read this book. It tells the story that is the closest to the heart of God, the story of redeeming love, compelling sacrifice and glorious good news."

— James T. Draper, Jr., President —
LifeWay Christian Resources of the Southern Baptist Convention

"Dub Jackson's vision of mobilizing thousands of volunteers to partner with missionaries and churches overseas was an idea ahead of its time but something that has become commonplace in mission strategies. This book is a testimony of God's blessing on a radical, innovative program that has accelerated global evangelization."

— Jerry Rankin, President —
International Mission Board, SBC

WHATEVER IT TAKES

Whatever it Takes

THE AMAZING
ADVENTURES
OF GOD'S WORK
AROUND THE WORLD

Dub Jackson

Broadman
&Holman
Publishers

NASHVILLE, TENNESSEE

0–8054–2688–4

Published by Broadman & Holman Publishers,
Nashville, Tennessee

Dewey Decimal Classification: 266
Subject Heading: MISSIONS \ EVANGELISTIC WORK

1 2 3 4 5 6 7 8 9 10 08 07 06 05 04 03

To God Be the Glory!

This book is an attempt to report on the many miracles and victories God has given over the past fifty years. All of the inspiration and everything of meaning and significance recorded here is the result of what the Lord has done. Thus, this book is dedicated with thanksgiving to our Lord and to our God.

CONTENTS

FOREWORD

DUB JACKSON WAS A PIONEER in an age of complacency. The prevailing philosophy of foreign missions was to send career missionaries to the nations of the world and let the fellow believers at home support them with their monies and prayers. Seldom was there a thought about visiting missionaries on their mission assignment. Long-distance phone calls were seldom used, even by those closest to the missionaries. Letters and reports took weeks to arrive back in the States. Business travelers were seldom in touch with missionaries on the field. Few ever thought about going to the field to assist in the work there. The philosophy of missions was simple: Tourists don't do missions. The work of fulfilling the Great Commission was left to those who served overseas and those who supported them. Seldom did the two groups meet.

Then Dub Jackson emerged on the scene in the 1950s. He envisioned great teams of volunteers coming to Japan, where he served. God planted a dream in his heart about reaching thousands of Japanese with the gospel of Jesus Christ. I remember vividly when he came to the Texas Baptist Evangelism Conference in the early 1960s and preached to the thousands present about the opportunity to reach Japan with the gospel. The result of his vision was the Japan New Life Crusade in 1963, when more than five hundred Texas Baptists went to Japan for a great crusade.

This book is about that watershed vision and the results that have multiplied exponentially since the 1950s in hundreds of crusades around the world. This is a book about miracles and divine provision. Routinely when plans would fall apart or when support would seem weak, God would intervene with events that could only be explained by the fact that God did them.

Dub's faithful partner in all of this is his wonderful wife, Doris. Few women would have followed their husband in such humanly impossible dreams. Yet without complaining, and never wavering in her love, prayers, and partnership in the vision, she has lived in a supernatural world of divine provision that always comes when one is abandoned to God and to God's will. Together Dub and Doris have charted a course for our day and the days to come. Because of their faithfulness, Partnership Missions is now a common name among Southern Baptists. Tens of thousands every year journey overseas to be part of that dream born in the heart of Dub Jackson.

This story must be told. Dub's simple conviction has been "Whatever it takes"—whatever it takes to share the gospel, whatever it takes to take God's people into the arenas of the world where the gospel can be preached in a different culture, whatever it takes to fulfill the dream is what we must give. That conviction has driven Dub and Doris over these fifty years. Only God knows how many times they have taken second mortgages on their homes to keep the dream alive. Never have they failed to take of their own funds to carry out a commitment. And through it all, never complaining about the sacrifice. And God has richly rewarded their efforts.

We are all recipients of their courage and conviction. At LifeWay alone, our mission teams that have gone out from this organization have seen over forty thousand professions of faith and over 130 churches begun in the first four years of our partnership efforts. And the same thing can be said of churches by the hundreds across our land. The dream is contagious, and thousands of Southern Baptists have joined Dub and Doris in their God-inspired dream.

This book is not a dull history of some business plan and its processes. This book is about the incredible moving of God in the lives of real people, people just like you and me. It is about the sacrifice that has brought now hundreds of thousands of people on partnership missions and millions into the kingdom of God through their witness. This book throbs with life and whets the appetite for more. Every born-again Christian ought to read this book. It tells the story that is the closest to the heart of God, the story of redeeming love, compelling sacrifice, and glorious good news.

These pages will drive you to your knees in self-examination. You will be compelled to ask, as I did, "Am I willing to do whatever it takes to follow the command of my Lord Jesus Christ?" To ask the question is to answer it. Yes, we will do whatever it takes! Dub and Doris have done what it takes, and they have blazed a trail for all of us to follow. Read these pages and weep, rejoice, and find yourself in a new surrender of life to our Lord. I commend these pages to you with great confidence in the presence of our Lord on every page.

Thank you, Dub and Doris, for your faithful service and your clear vision of the dream God planted in your hearts.
In His love,

— James T. Draper, Jr. —

PREFACE

THIS BOOK REPORTS MANY OF THE MIRACLES and victories God has given over the past fifty years. All of the inspiration and everything of meaning and significance recorded here is the result of what the Lord has done. This book is an expression of thanksgiving to Him for the joy and victories He gave as we witnessed around the world.

After more than fifty years of combined missionary service, ministry, and Partnership Evangelism, there is more to share than can be put in one book. For every victory we have recorded here, there are a hundred we have not mentioned! Our prayer is that the reader will be reminded that God is always able to do all things, anywhere, anytime when we believe and ask in faith.

Whatever else may result from reading this book, I pray that God will be honored and that we will be convinced that He can and will use us if we will ask Him.

Finally, we pray that if the reader has never received Christ as Lord, he will know that His salvation and forgiveness are available right now, *just for the asking!*

ACKNOWLEDGMENTS

IT IS IMPOSSIBLE TO RECOGNIZE ALL who have made contributions to the work described here, but I want to thank some who helped in the early days when Partnership seemed impossible. K. Owen White, Ramsey Pollard, T. A. Patterson, C. Wade Freeman, Herschel Hobbs, Shuichi Matsumura and Mrs. Matsumura, and others, were there when the vision and challenge began. Jimmy and Carol Ann Draper have been amazing and unfailing in their support and encouragement. In the days before Southern Baptists fully understood Partnership, Dr. Draper led, advised, and believed in Partnership, leading the First Baptist Church of Euless, Texas, to contribute ten thousand dollars a year, until Partnership became an accepted and effective arm of Southern Baptists to reach the world!

A very special thank you is due Ruth Halvarson, friend and missionary to Japan, who has transcribed all the victories recorded here.

Billy and Vivian Marie Keith gave great help in editing portions of the book. Their help has been more than professional, for our friendship began as missionaries together many years ago in Japan.

Jerry and Fran McIver have cared for our personal responsibilities while we have been overseas. Without their invaluable help, we could not have been away to coordinate Partnership Campaigns.

Carol Cost has carried the office responsibilities for our Partnerships for many years. She has been a faithful and dedicated servant of the Lord who understands Partnership.

We wish to thank our many friends overseas. John and Robert Casagrande of Luzerne, Switzerland, gladly cooperated, and John even provided his computer when ours crashed in Europe. Patrice Glogg, general manager of the Burgenstock Hotel in Luzerne; Herbert Mosbruck, general manager of the Salzburg Sheraton in Austria; and Michael Schuetzendorf of the Hilton Corporation in Germany, provided space for work away from home when we could pause to record these miracles.

A very special thanks to Broadman & Holman Publishers, and especially to Leonard Goss and John Landers for the tremendous job they have done in editing and arranging my material to let the inspiration and message be clearly understood. Thanks also to Paul Mikos and the marketing staff.

Roy Workman, copy supervisor at OfficeMax, Abilene, Texas, has been ever present in making sure I could see in hard copy what had been put on the computer.

HIS WINGS OVER MY WINGS

WORLD WAR II WAS RAGING throughout the
South Pacific the day I drove my Jeep
toward a little airstrip deep in the hot,
steamy jungles of Nadzab, New
Guinea. That was to be a day of
serious preparation for reentering
combat as a fighter pilot. It was also
going to be the first of many days
the Lord would use to prepare and
preserve me for the work He had
planned. The Nadzab airstrip had
been laid out along the Markham Valley
between the mountains of the Owen
Stanley Range, where all pilots and combat
crews took familiarization flights before going
into combat.

*In primary
flight training*

Nadzab was secure, but most of the island was still held by
the Japanese, and our daily missions consisted of dive-bombing
and strafing targets in and around Wewak and Rabul. Other

Chapter 1

planes involved in these missions were the B–24 and B–25 bombers, together with P–47 and P–51 fighters. Of course I was overjoyed as my Jeep pulled up in front of the choice of almost every young pilot I knew, the world-famous Lockheed P–38, the fastest fighter in the world!

My heart beat with anticipation that morning as I approached the primitive hut we called the Operations Center. Fifth Air Force Fighter Command in the Philippines had just assigned me to fly P–38s with the Forty-ninth Fighter Group! It was a dream come true! After years of longing to fly America's number one fighter plane, *today* I would make my solo flight in the P–38!

There were no P–38 instructors at this advanced combat staging area, so we were given tech orders for the plane and told to study them until we were ready to fly. My good friend Bill Hamilton was also transferring to fighters and joined with me as we took the tech manuals and studied them all morning. By one o'clock we felt ready to give it a try, so we drove back to the strip and declared to the major that we were ready to go. He pointed to two beautiful P–38s parked in front of Operations and said, "Take 'em up, and from here on you are on your own!" That was our formal training for combat flying in the P–38.

I started the two powerful Allison engines and taxied onto the runway, pushed the throttles forward, and held the brakes until the plane vibrated into full power. When I released the brakes, the plane shot down the runway and up into the New Guinea sky. I was weeping for joy as I looked out and saw those beautiful blue-and-white Air Force markings on the wing and realized my dream had come true. This had to be one of the greatest days of my life as a pilot, for nothing had been more important to me than serving my country and flying that P–38.

In the cockpit of my P–38 before a combat mission
Philippines, 1945

A fighter was unlike any of the planes I had flown before. In a fighter you could roll, dive, and loop as you pleased, while as a bomber pilot, it was just straight and level! This was real flying! The plane was easy to handle, and I flew about seventy-five miles over the jungles and the tall kuni grass and began practicing peel-ups in order to be ready to make a real fighter approach when I came back to Nadzab for my first landing. While flying back to Nadzab to land, I dipped down just above the grass, and at 350 MPH, I was impressed to pray, "Lord, when this war is over, and if You spare me to return home, should I do something that would dishonor Your name, I would rather You just cut one of these engines now!" Although that was not the kind of prayer the Lord wanted to hear, I held my breath, for I really meant it! When the field came into view, I crossed the end of the runway, still at 350 mph, and chopped the throttles, pulling up into a climbing 360-degree turn to kill off speed and put down my wheels and flaps. Twenty seconds later, after an approach that was almost a loop, I touched down in what would always be my favorite airplane, the P–38. I was thrilled speechless. I had just flown America's number one fighter!

A Never-to-Be-Forgotten Emergency!

One week later on March 15, 1945, a day I will remember forever, God in His great mercy preserved me in spite of my inexperience and mistakes in flying. On that day I had gone to the Operations Center to check out my plane for additional transition in preparation for combat. I needed to cram in as much flight training as possible in order to be ready to join the fighter group that had invited me to fly with them. It was another beautiful morning, and I can still see my plane poised and ready for flight. The sergeant informed me that my plane had been outfitted for combat, and the four fifty-caliber machine guns and the twenty-millimeter canon were fully armed. As I climbed up on the wing to get into the cockpit, I also saw two five-hundred-pound bombs hanging under the wing. Since the combat mission had been cancelled, the sergeant told me to jettison the bombs in the river after takeoff. His last remarks were, "Oh, by the way, pay no attention to that left fuel gauge—it doesn't work."

I would soon discover that this flight would be one of the most exciting and nerve-racking of my short life! The takeoff was routine, and as I soared higher and higher through the light, fluffy clouds that usually turned into rain in the afternoon, the peaks of the Owen Stanley Range came quickly into focus. Today I planned to practice flying with one engine dead. I shut down the right engine and began flying on the left one, with one propeller feathered. I had been practicing single-engine procedures for about forty-five minutes when a string of P–47s and P–51s cut in front of me and pulled up into what we called a "rat race" or a game like follow-the-leader. I decided to get in on the fun so restarted the dead engine and pulled hard on the controls to join in with them. Suddenly my plane made a violent roll to the left. I thought that sudden maneuver had been caused by one of the combat flaps failing to come down. Since the plane had flown smoothly on one engine with one prop feathered, I just did not associate this problem with a dead engine. However, I knew I was in big trouble!

I was too far from my home field to return, so I pulled the nose up to climb over the mountains and to attempt an emergency landing on the other side at Lae, New Guinea, an Australian field. As I struggled to maintain control of the plane, I remembered that Lae was the last airfield from which the famed aviatrix Amelia Earhart had flown before disappearing during her attempt to fly around the world.

With my P–38 Lockheed Lightning

As I climbed over the mountains, losing valuable air speed and almost losing directional control, I called the tower at Lae and informed them that I was coming in for an emergency landing. The Australian controller cleared me to land but instructed me to approach the field from the ocean toward the mountains.

I radioed back that because of the emergency, I would have to land the best way I could. Normally I would approach the landing strip at about 110 mph and touch down at eighty-five or ninety. But because of my emergency, I found that I had to fly at 165 mph to maintain directional control! I was losing airspeed all along as I climbed to clear the tops of the mountains, and just before the plane would have stalled and rolled over into the ground, I topped the mountain and quickly pushed the nose down to pick up airspeed and regain control. At this point I could see the Lae field clearly and understood immediately why the tower had instructed me to approach the field from the ocean! From a mountain approach, I would have to pull up to clear an electric power line and be forced to land further down the already-too-short runway, thus giving up some valuable runway that I would need in order to stop the plane before crashing into the ocean.

After clearing the power lines, I decided to push the nose down and force the plane onto the muddy field with my brakes locked. I figured that would cause my nose gear to collapse, and help me stop before going into the ocean. When I hit the ground, the plane slid sideways at a high speed, then leaped back into the air. I pushed it back on the wet ground again, with the brakes still locked, dirt and mud flying everywhere.

My priority shifted quickly from trying to save the plane to surviving without going into the ocean! Having been raised in west Texas, where water was always scarce, I didn't know how to swim and was determined to stop the plane before it hit the water.

The plane began to skid and swerve toward the tower as I tried to hold it straight, and when I reached the end of the runway with mud and dirt still flying, I released one brake and let the plane spin around until it stopped just short of the ocean. The Australians in the tower later told me that when the plane veered toward them they were about ready to bail out of the tower and run for safety.

When the propeller on the dead engine stopped turning, I realized what had happened—the tank with the inoperative fuel gauge had run out of gas! Flying with one dead engine and a prop that had not been feathered had forced me to fly at a high rate of speed in order to keep control.

That day, flying over the jungles of New Guinea, I broke every rule of self-preservation in landing the plane with one engine out. But God had preserved me anyway!

I sat in the cockpit, as the dust settled, and thanked the Lord for His care. I was still sitting there when the Australians drove up in their Jeep. I climbed down out of the plane and immediately realized just how much care God had given. Under the wings were the bombs I had forgotten to jettison! Had I been successful in collapsing the gear, the plane would have been blown to bits! That was an amazing and miraculous rescue from disaster. God was there.

God Takes Care Again!

On a night bombing mission from Clark Field in the Philippines to the Japanese-held Ten Ho airfield in Canton, China, we were to be faced with another urgent need for God's care as the searchlights and antiaircraft guns zeroed in on us, and Japanese fighters followed us from the target.

At that time I was assigned to a squadron of B–24s of the Forty-third Bomb Group, of the Fifth Air Force. Our missions were usually designed to find and bomb enemy ships. We always flew at night and at low altitude. One evening we took off from Clark Field just at dusk, flying low and through the night, headed for our first checkpoint, Hong Kong. As we approached this Japanese-held city, our plane set off alarms, and the Japanese began turning off all their lights. By the time we were over the city, all was dark!

By radar we picked up the Pearl River out of Hong Kong and flew toward the target at four thousand feet altitude. The Japanese soon spotted us, and their searchlights were so bright I could have read a newspaper in the cockpit. We took our propellers out of synchronization and began to fly in an evasive pattern, trying to get away from their lights and guns. The crew members threw out the radar window, which is a tinfoil type material designed to throw off track radar-controlled lights and antiaircraft guns. Nothing seemed to help. We were firmly fixed in their lights!

As a last resort, we tried an old trick that had been successful before. The waist gunners began throwing out empty beer bottles they had brought along for that purpose. The whistle of these empty bottles made so much noise the Japanese below assumed we were dropping bombs and turned off their lights.

We continued up the river to our initial checkpoint, turned right, and proceeded to methodically and repeatedly bomb Ten Ho airfield. On the last run over the airdrome, we dropped a string of bombs right down the runway, then turned for home.

Just out of Hong Kong, the tail gunner called and said that we had Japanese night fighters crisscrossing our tail. However, as they prepared to attack, we flew into some thick clouds that I have to believe God prepared for us, and we were able to return safely to our base in the Philippines.

I never cease to give thanks to God for His constant care. Clearly on this flight and every flight in World War II, I firmly believe that He preserved my life for the missionary service He later called us to. I could not have imagined all of the spiritual joys, battles, and victories He was going to give to us in our missionary service and witness to the Japanese who were so aggressively seeking to destroy us!

Through the above illustrations of God's care and leading and through other numerous and continued instances of His care, God directed us into the most joyous and victorious life one could have ever dreamed of! Thank God for His plan and purpose for our lives.

WORLD WAR II ENDS—SPIRITUAL CHALLENGES MULTIPLY

EVENTUALLY THE JAPANESE IMPERIAL ARMY was defeated, and General Douglas MacArthur accepted Japan's surrender on the battleship *Missouri* on September 2, 1945, in Tokyo Bay.

Our fighter group, because of the record they had set throughout the war, was selected to enter Japan with General MacArthur as his honor guard. Thus we were among the first to land in Japan following the war. I was not one of the heroes of the Forty-ninth but had volunteered for every mission, and my squadron commander, Major James Watkins, had just made me operations officer for our Seventh Squadron. When I had requested transfer from bombers to fighters, I had promised him that if he approved, I was willing to stay overseas until the war was over! At that time, the atomic bomb had not been dropped, and it looked like a long, long war. At any rate, our planes were the first to land in Japan, and God was giving me a head start on my coming missionary opportunities.

Chapter 2

Our occupation assignment was to patrol the country, looking for signs of any factories still in operation or of any resistance. From the beginning of the occupation, God also began to give me wonderful opportunities to serve and represent Him, as well as my country.

Several of us started going to the Yokohama GI Gospel Hour, where I had the joy of sharing my testimony and playing the trumpet I had taken overseas with me. We met in Yokohama in a little chapel on the south pier, and it was filled to capacity every Saturday night. All the men who attended had fought their way through the jungles and islands of the South Pacific and were thrilled to be alive and able to sing and give thanks to God for the victory and His protection.

Paul Goercke, a merchant seaman, was the pianist, and in my opinion, one of the greatest pianists I had ever heard. I do not remember ever being in services with more Spirit-filled gospel singing. Chaplains, officers, and men who had found Christ to be real during the war were in charge and brought the messages.

The Yokohama meetings went so well we decided to organize the Tokyo GI Gospel Hour in the Ginza Methodist Church in Tokyo. The church had been bombed out during the war, and our first meetings were held in their auditorium with the rebuilding, scaffolding, and scars of war all around. God greatly used everyone in those days to let us share His love with the defeated Japanese and to prepare many of us for future missionary service.

I thank God for those GI Gospel Hour meetings! We will always have a special love and appreciation for them and for an organization called Youth for Christ. They responded more quickly and readily with the gospel for Japan than any other Christian organization at that time. Their valuable and timely ministry was effective and blessed by God for the salvation of thousands of Japanese and by giving the major denominations time to gear up and begin making the contribution that only they could make. Baptists and other Christians should never cease to give thanks to God for the more mobile and aggressive smaller organizations that contributed so much in the early days in Japan.

As the GIs ministered in those days, Japan was in ruins, but Japanese hearts were open to the gospel and hungry for a message of hope. When the emperor surrendered, the Japanese had to acknowledge that he was not divine. The morale of the country was zero. They had lost not only the war but also their hope for the future.

Wherever we went, we were constantly reminded of the destruction that was all about us and of the despair and defeat that was in the hearts of the people. While driving my Jeep from Atsugi to Yokohama and Tokyo, I saw little but smokestacks, rusted safes, and burned-out buildings in every direction. Both cities were flattened, and there was nothing but trash and rubble. There were only a few vehicles still operating, and I can remember driving in Tokyo when my Jeep was the only vehicle on the streets.

Death in the Tunnels

On one occasion Ugo Nakada, a great Christian music leader, guided me through the Shinjuku Railroad Station on our way to a special meeting. That train station was and still is one of the busiest in all of Asia. Mr. Nakada explained that after Tokyo was destroyed, people poured into the station every night to find some protection from the cold and to sleep on the wet tile floors in the tunnels beneath the station.

We walked through, carefully tiptoeing over women and children who had gathered early to find a place to sleep that night.

Mr. Nakada reminded me, "In the morning, our American soldiers will back their trucks up to the station entrance, and stretcher bearers will come in and carry out those who have died of exposure and starvation."

Today, as we look at the modern, aggressive, economic giant that is Japan, it is hard to realize that such a day ever existed. Just as my Jeep was sometimes the only vehicle in sight during those days, it seemed that our message was also the only one available. It was a day of great need!

On the very first Sunday Tokyo was opened to military personnel, Roger Fox, a pilot friend of mine, went with me into Tokyo in search of a well-known Japanese pastor named Toyohiko Kagawa. We had no idea where he lived, but I carried a note with his name written in Japanese and showed it to several people as we sought directions. God finally led us down a little alley in the Shinjuku area of Tokyo to the Kagawa Fellowship Home.

A worship service was in progress as we arrived. We took off our shoes, as was the custom in Japan, and sat down to listen to Dr. Kagawa preach. I was embarrassed to notice that I had holes in my socks.

After the service, he introduced us to the congregation and gave us an opportunity to share a greeting as we met with the Japanese Christians. I've often wondered what that little group must have thought when Roger and I, who had been their enemies only a few days before, walked into their service and were introduced to them as their guests.

After meeting Dr. Kagawa, we also had the unexpected joy of meeting six American women missionaries who had just been released from a Japanese concentration camp the week before. All of them were older than sixty, and one was eighty-two!

My impressions and challenges for mission service really began when I met those wonderful missionaries who had been imprisoned during the war. The time spent with them was used to burn into my heart the need for a witness to a nation that had been both physically and spiritually destroyed.

Meeting those godly missionaries was one of the greatest experiences of my life. They had faithfully served the Lord throughout the war, even while in prison. Although they have long since passed from this life, I will never forget them or their names. There was Helen Topping, an eighty-two-year-old American Baptist missionary; Betty Kilburn, a Presbyterian; Ann Devendorf and Mabel Frances, Christian and Missionary Alliance; and Ruth Ward, a Methodist.

Several weeks after meeting these missionaries, I arranged to take Helen Topping—Mother Tops, as we called her—to the Tachikawa Air Base to speak to a hangar filled with Air Force personnel. It was a cold and rainy day in December, and my open Jeep bounced along the bomb-marked road.

I said to her, "Mother Tops, I feel like I'm killing you, taking you out in this cold, rainy weather in an open Jeep and over these terrible roads."

She looked at me and smiled and said, "Young man, it is not the cold on the outside that keeps us from going or serving. It is the cold on the inside!" Their faithful witness under very trying circumstances was a never-to-be-forgotten lesson in how to serve and keep on serving!

At about this time I asked my squadron commander, Major James Watkins, for permission to use military vehicles to help these missionary friends when we had free time. We assured him we still recognized our military duty and would not miss any of the assigned surveillance flights. The major replied, "Take off whenever you are free and use any vehicle we have on the base to do what you think needs to be done." Major Watkins was sympathetic to our desire to help the missionaries and knew we would not shirk our flying responsibilities in the occupation. I never lost my love for flying, but I had a growing concern for the missionaries and mission work.

God used our time in the Japanese occupation to open my eyes to the physical and spiritual needs of the country and begin leading me to think of going back to help them spiritually. I knew that defeating the Japanese military was an absolute must, but I also recognized that we had the good news of God's love that the people of Japan desperately needed in their darkest hour.

Soon after arriving in Japan and with the help of Chaplain Pate, a Southern Baptist minister from Texas, we organized an evangelistic meeting for Atsugi, the city near our home base, where General MacArthur and the first occupation planes had landed.

The Atsugi meeting was my first experience at setting up a large evangelistic campaign. We asked for and received the support of the mayor, the city council, and high school officials, and we received permission to have the meeting in the high school auditorium, the only building of any size still standing in the city.

On the night of the meeting, the building was completely filled. Roger and I shared our testimonies, I played the trumpet, and Chaplain Pate preached.

When the invitation was given, every person in the building slid forward on that tatami floor, indicating a desire to know Christ. We were afraid they did not understand the invitation, so we gave it again and made it clear that this was asking them to seek forgiveness through Christ and to give themselves to Him. Again, every person in the building slid forward, indicating their desire to accept Christ. It was clear that there could not be any place in all the world where the people were more open and anxious to find the answer to their empty lives!

Shortly after that experience, I located a Japanese quartermaster depot that, although locked, had great stores of blankets and winter underwear. The war was over, and those blankets were not being used. Roger and I broke the locks on the building and loaded an army truck with the life-saving valuable cargo. We headed for the missionary fellowship home where Mabel Frances joined us and guided us to a Buddhist temple, where many of Tokyo's most needy people were gathered for shelter.

Tokyo had been completely destroyed during firebomb raids on May 25, and more people had been killed in those raids than had been killed in the atomic blast at Hiroshima. On one night in May, more than 250,000 Japanese had perished in what was the most destructive single-night air raid in the history of modern warfare.

Mabel Frances guided us through that destruction to a Buddhist temple where only people with absolutely nothing were permitted to stay. Those destitute people had somehow been alerted to our coming and were anxiously awaiting our arrival.

We drove our truck onto the temple grounds and immediately began distributing the blankets and underwear. As we prepared to depart, a man came running up to us carrying a hat filled to overflowing with Japanese yen. We learned this was an offering taken up from those who had absolutely nothing! It was a thank-you for the blankets and clothes!

We gave the offering to the missionaries and turned the truck around and slowly drove away. When we looked back to wave good-bye, all the Japanese were sitting on the ground in neat lines facing our truck with their heads bowed to the ground! They remained in that position until we were out of sight!

Remembering those people there that night, I drove back toward our base with a burden the Lord would never take away! I can see it as clearly today as when we were there.

On another occasion we were invited by the Mitsui family to go to their country home outside of Tokyo and witness concerning Christ. Little did we know that the Mitsui family was and is today one of the three richest families in all Japan. The financial power of these three families had prompted General MacArthur to divide their holdings in order to strip them of their monopolistic economic and military power. We had a great time of sharing that afternoon, and one of the Mitsui daughters joyfully accepted Christ as Lord and Savior. It was just another amazing day among many that God gave in those early days in defeated Japan.

We learned that the Mitsui country home where we visited had been set aside for the entertainment of the Kamikazi pilots before their final missions.

The Lord used every opportunity to impress upon me the needs of this physically and spiritually hungry people. I was impressed over and over with the need to share Christ with Japan immediately!

On Christmas Eve in 1945 we were invited to go with the missionaries to a school for the blind near the Kagawa Fellowship Home. It was a beautiful, crisp, cold night, and the school, as was true with most homes and buildings in that day, was without any heat. We joined several missionaries who were leading that Christmas service and were sharing their faith. I gave my testimony through an interpreter and again played my trumpet. I will never forget the nearness of Christ in that school for the blind in that cold building on Christmas Eve 1945! After the testimonies and preaching, when the invitation was given, many of those blind students raised their hands saying they wanted to accept Christ as Savior.

In remembering the first Christmas in Japan following the war, I have to recall a special hour with Dr. Kagawa. I was invited to go with him to play my trumpet as he brought the first post-war Christmas message for the students and faculty at the Imperial University in Tokyo.

Ugo Nakada guided me to the university for the program, and he led the beautiful Christmas music in that historic service as Dr. Kagawa preached! It was a special day, and I was grateful for the opportunity of being a part of such a service. I played "The Holy City" on my trumpet in what was surely the least-holy city on earth at the time.

Every day in Japan, God was giving me a deeper conviction that people without a church, without the message of Christ, and without hope must be given the opportunity to know of the love and joy that only Christ can give. Although I had not personally felt a call to return as a missionary, I determined to go back to the United States and do everything I could to rally support to make sure the message of salvation through Christ would be taken to Japan.

In January 1946 as I prepared to leave Japan, I drove to the Kagawa Fellowship Home to say thank you and good-bye. With all the joy of a twenty-one-year old about to be going

In full uniform

home, I called to Mabel Frances, one of the missionaries, and said, "I'm going home. Don't you want to go with me?" I'll never forget her reply, "I am home!"

Driving back to my base as I contemplated my return to the United States, all of those experiences God had given flooded through my mind. I remembered the many times when we had taken army canned goods to the missionaries and the truckloads of scrap lumber we had given to them to fight the cold of that first winter. I remembered the many occasions when I had driven down the narrow alley leading to the missionary home and had seen the empty GI food cans in all the trash boxes along the way. The missionaries had been feeding the whole neighborhood with the food we had brought to them. We had seen an amazing expression of love and devotion for the Japanese people during the days of the occupation. I had the great privilege of seeing love in action, and I will remember it for as long as I live. Surely that is one of the reasons that today, fifty-seven years later, I am in the midst of setting up eleven more evangelistic campaigns for Tokyo and Asahigawa for next year. The love, the vision, and the burden for Japan that the Lord gave in 1945 has increased every year.

I have often thought that after World War II, Baptists alone could have accepted General MacArthur's challenge to send ten thousand missionaries to Japan. Had we done so, we could be talking about a Christian nation today! So far as I can remember, Southern Baptists, the largest evangelical denomination in the world, never had more than two hundred missionaries in Japan at any one time.

We have all heard stories of the great open doors for the gospel of Jesus Christ in certain lands, but whatever we may have heard, there could never have been a country more open to the gospel than was Japan following World War II. We must confess that we failed to accept the challenge God gave to us for Japan. We did not give Japan what we could have given, what they requested, and what God expected us to give. We do thank the Lord for what did take place and for the efforts that were made. Yet how small it was compared with what we could have done in response to that challenge! I am confident that had we recognized the challenge and presented it to our people, Christians would have gladly given whatever was needed to see the message of hope and salvation shared in Japan while the door was open.

I will always be thankful to the Lord for taking me to Japan in World War II. He used that to prepare me and introduce me to the great missionary challenge of that country and of the whole world. Thank the Lord, today we can be introduced to world needs through Partnership Evangelism instead of through war!

TO JAPAN ON A PRAYER

IN THE SUMMER OF 1950, while I was pastoring a small mission in Mineral Wells, Texas, and attending Southwestern Seminary, Edwin Dozier, the senior missionary in Japan, invited Theron "Corky" Farris and seven of us to go to Japan to help in a summer of evangelism. We were students and none of us had *any* money! Those were the days when it was very unusual for anyone other than appointed missionaries to go overseas to serve. There was nothing in the entire world that I wanted to do more than get back to Japan and preach, but it seemed impossible. There was *no* money and none in sight, and we had only six weeks before the scheduled departure. I was making only fifty dollars a month and would have to resign the church in order to go, thus stopping what little income we had. How could I go and how could Doris and our two-year-old son live while I was away? It was not a reasonable plan, and it certainly looked impossible!

My first response was no. Thank the Lord the invitation came again, and this time they said, "We must have you to serve as one of the preachers." There were to be three teams—Corky Farris, Bill Crook, and me as preachers. Henry Ikemoto was to go as an interpreter, and David Appleby, Doug Dillard, and Earl Miller as musicians. Earl was a tremendous pianist from First Baptist Church in Dallas, and David Appleby was an accomplished pianist and a talented musician who had been born on a mission field in South America. Doug was a multitalented person who could preach as well as sing.

Before we made our final decision, we agreed to meet in the back of Gambrell Street Baptist Church to pray and seek the Lord's leading. Our situation had not changed, but we all came away from that prayer meeting with a clear leading to go to Japan in spite of the circumstances. Yet the Foreign Mission Board advised us not to go, and my favorite seminary professor, Cal Guy, also advised us not to go. He said, "In light of the Foreign Mission Board's stand concerning this trip and your desire to be appointed as a missionary next year, I think you may need to reconsider your decision." What a difficult dilemma!

In my entire ministry from my first invitation to preach in New Mexico until today, I have always believed that if I am free, I must go. In an effort to explain my conviction to Baker James Cauthen, the Foreign Mission Board's executive secretary, I took a space-available flight on an Air Force plane to Chicago to meet and talk with him. It was June 1950, and I wanted personally to assure Dr. Cauthen that our Japan campaign was the result of a positive decision we had made after receiving the invitation to go. Dr. Cauthen was preaching for the Southern Baptist Convention's annual meeting, and after his message one evening we met near the front of the auditorium. I explained to him that Edwin Dozier, a veteran missionary in Japan, had invited us to come and help, and we had agreed to go. Although sympathetic, Dr. Cauthen could not give me any encouragement and stood firm in his conviction that no students should participate in campaigns in Japan at that time. This was only five years after the war, and there were still many physical needs in Japan. I returned to Fort Worth disappointed and concerned that if we followed our convictions to go, our board might not appoint us as missionaries the following year.

Nevertheless, I resigned my church and began in earnest making preparations. The cost of participation was about sixteen hundred dollars, an astronomical amount in those days for a student with no money! I moved Doris and our two-year-old son, Billy, to Abilene to stay with my parents while I was away. Doris went back to work at Citizens National Bank as I began trying to raise funds. We were following a principle I believed to be biblical, then and now: do everything we can, and trust the Lord to do the rest. I wrote to a number of friends, asking them if they would consider helping with the financial support. Never having participated in anything that required financial assistance before, I did not know how to go about raising the funds. I shared the need with my family and a few of the members of my first country church, but when it came time to depart, we were still considerably short of our goal. A used-car dealer in Fort Worth came to our rescue and provided three used cars for us to drive to San Francisco, and paid us fifty dollars each to drive them. We looked upon this as just another miracle among many the Lord gave in connection with that campaign.

We left for the west coast, still far short of our fund-raising goal. I remember receiving some special love gifts from the B. W. Bakers and the W. H. Mays, members of my father's former church in Wilson, Texas. Mother and Dad were not blessed with wealth, having spent their lives pastoring small country churches, but they sacrificially gave from their meager resources.

I have thanked the Lord many times for that experience. He led us to go overseas on a campaign when there was no money and seemingly no possible way to go! He showed us how *He could provide* and give a victory when all seemed impossible, even when there were only a few days to do what usually takes a year or more to do. *Because of that experience, I have been able to stand before people in large and small churches alike and assure them that if God leads them to participate, He will provide all they need when they need it! Their abilities or financial status have nothing to do with what He can do.* That summer crusade made it possible for me to challenge people, regardless of their circumstances, to accept whatever challenge He sets before them. *Our task* always is to trust and launch out on faith when He says go!

We experienced some humorous moments as we left Fort Worth for the West Coast and Japan, driving our three used cars. It was interesting to see the shocked expression on the service station attendants' faces when they learned that we were headed for Japan and missionary work. One of our cars was a bright yellow Chrysler convertible, and the laughing and joyous young men dressed in T-shirts and baseball caps did not fit the image they had of missionaries. I don't think those attendants ever believed that we were headed for the mission field. The world always seems to expect a missionary to be sad, but there is no more joyous life in the world than that of being in the center of God's will, doing what He wants us to do! It cannot be matched. I have a deep conviction that God gives a special joy to those who are involved in sharing His love with those who have never before had the opportunity to hear.

Whether witnessing in a student crusade or in Partnership campaigns, we learned that we could always be sure of three things:

1. Most participants will say, "It has been the greatest joy of my life."

2. We will have a constant battle with Satan when we accept frontline duty.

3. We can always be sure of victory! God never leads His people into defeat. The victories come in many forms, but there are always victories.

That was certainly true in 1950. If you should happen to have copies of your old 1950 newspapers, you will note that a shipping strike broke out on the west coast and halted all ship movements that summer! We had planned to travel to Japan by freighter because that was the least expensive mode of travel. Our sixteen-hundred-dollar cost was based on traveling to and from Japan in this way. When we learned of the strike, we knelt on our knees and asked God to open a door. In one of those prayer meetings, one of our group said, "God told us to go; He did not tell us to come back!" Thus we decided to buy a one-way airplane ticket to Japan, using all of the funds we had collected. Time was rapidly slipping by, and we felt an urgency to get to Japan as quickly as possible.

Taking all our luggage and equipment, we went early the next morning to the San Francisco International Airport and began checking in at the United Airlines desk. We had two portable organs, three wire recorders, a trumpet, an accordion, and all sorts of equipment that we could have put on a ship easily! But our switch to the plane left us with more excess baggage than we could ever have hoped to take. Even the best four-engine propeller aircraft of that day had critical weight limits, unlike the jets of today. Airlines were especially careful about weight on their long over-water flights. We went up to the counter with all of our luggage and equipment, and the man behind the desk said, "Did you know that whatever you have on will not be counted against your weight allowance?"

With his instructions, we opened our bags and began to repack, right there in full view of the amazed occupants in the rotunda of the San Francisco International Airport. We put on coats and filled our pockets with everything we could stuff in them. When we had finished, we waddled back up to the check-in counter and, by now, a different man greeted us with the announcement, "You are three hundred dollars over on your weight allowance." What a blow! There we were with no money, and we began to think of all our wasted effort. Could it be that we had come this far to be stopped by a three-hundred-dollar excess baggage charge? We told the man that we did not have three hundred dollars. He asked us, "Why are you going to Japan?" We told him that we were going, at the invitation of a missionary, for evangelistic campaigns planned for that summer. He paused a moment and, as we held our breath, then said, "This will be on United Airlines. Welcome aboard!" Our hearts nearly burst with joy as we saw the Lord perform yet another miracle. After checking in, we went over to a quiet place near the public telephones in that rotunda and thanked God for taking care of our problem, and we asked Him to forgive us for our lack of faith! We were reminded again that God is always able.

Our plane arrived in Honolulu too late to make our connections with Pan American and our flight to Tokyo. We were handed a mimeographed letter apologizing for the delay and telling us we would have to wait three days for the next flight. The layover arrangements did not cause us to complain. We would have to wait in a hotel on Waikiki beach for three days for the next flight to Japan. The airline representative explained, "We will provide the lodging and all of your meals while you wait!" As a group of seminary students accustomed to living in poverty, we said, "Please don't worry about it. We will struggle through!" There we were, trying to go to Japan by freighter, and the Lord was letting us fly and providing us with a three-day paid vacation on Waikiki Beach! Amazing!

On our departure day for Tokyo, we boldly took our luggage to the Pan American check-in counter and trusted the Lord to provide another miracle! As the agent weighed our bags, he simply said, "You know you are overweight," and we answered, "Yes, sir." Then he said, "We will take care of it." God had provided again. Even in the days of strict weight regulations, we were able to go on to Tokyo on schedule.

Upon arrival in Japan, we immediately began witnessing and sharing in the heart of Tokyo. One of the outstanding experiences of that summer took place in the Shibuya railroad station as we stood on the hood of a Jeep, witnessing and handing out tracts. Literally hundreds of people had gathered at the sound of my trumpet, and they remained to hear the message and to receive the salvation tracts. They had gathered in their tattered olive-drab clothes and in their wooden shoes (*geta*), without socks, and eagerly listened to the message of hope we shared with them in that day of defeat. The economy we associate with Japan today was completely missing in 1950. They had nothing! As we handed out the salvation tracts, all we could see were hands reaching up. We could feel people tugging at our clothes, saying in broken English, "Me one, sir! Me one. Me one?" To this day, I can still see those hands and hear those voices begging for help!

In another meeting at the Shibuya railroad station, Dr. Wagner of Pocket Testament League had handed a tract to one of those men reaching and clutching for the gospels. That man had prayed to receive the Lord, and we had invited him to join with us in a street meeting in Nagoya a few days later. That young man was none other than Commander Mitsuo Fuchida, the pilot who had led the attack on Pearl Harbor in 1941! He was the pilot who had radioed back to the aircraft carrier, *"Tora! Tora! Tora!"* signifying a successful surprise attack.

The street meeting in front of the Nagoya railroad station on that rainy afternoon was a memorable one! There I was, an ex-fighter pilot, standing next to the Japanese pilot who had led the attack on Pearl Harbor, and we were both sharing our testimonies concerning the love of Christ and the salvation He had given to us. From the top of our Chevrolet panel truck, I played my trumpet and Commander Fuchida and I gave our testimonies before Dave Morken, of Youth for Christ, preached a salvation message. When the invitation was given, hundreds of Japanese knelt in the rain and mud and prayed to receive Christ as Lord. After the service we returned to a little Japanese inn where we spent the night. I slept with my back against the paper *shoji* wall, realizing that on the other side of that paper wall slept our former enemy and the leader of the Pearl Harbor attack, Commander Fuchida! *Is this not amazing grace!*

Years later, in January 1961, after I had spoken for the Texas Baptist Evangelism Conference at First Baptist Church in Dallas, Commander Fuchida came up to me and told me that he, too, had become a preacher of the gospel. He was a faithful minister until his death a few years ago. Surely, "all things are possible to him that believeth."

One of the last of the many meetings we had in Japan was in Tokyo's Ikebukuro railroad station. In the dust and dirt of post-war Japan, we shared our testimonies in music and message and extended the invitation. The shadows of dusk made it difficult for us to see as we sought to talk with those who had raised their hands to indicate they would like to know Christ as Savior. One young man was struggling to find the Lord as I counseled with him. In the darkness he had turned on his bicycle headlight so that we could read the Scripture together. Finally I asked him to indicate what his decision had been. He paused and looked up at me in the shadows of that bicycle headlight and said, "I have no money. Can I be a Christian?" What a joy to tell him that the price had already been paid in full by the death of Christ our Savior and that his salvation was a free gift! Jesus had said, "Ask, and you shall receive." With joy and new energy, this young man eagerly signed the decision card, saying he had accepted Christ as his Savior! That was typical of the many hundreds of experiences God gave that summer. We thanked Him that He had led us to Japan and had enabled us to go.

After six weeks of evangelistic campaigns from Shikoku to Hokkaido, I had my last service in Hiroshima on a Sunday night. I had just preached in a Christian and Missionary Alliance church across the boulevard from the home of Southern Baptist missionaries Curtis and Mary Lee Askew. I walked back to their house through the still-fresh rubble of the atomic blast of 1945, reflecting on the fact that even as an American, I had been able to share the message of Christ's love with those who had just experienced the horrors of that destruction. Many had come to know Christ as Savior, and I was still rejoicing. When I approached the gates of the Askew home, Mary Lee rushed out and said what we all thought would be true: World War III had just started! The Korean War had exploded that day, and we all expected the next conflict to be nuclear and to result in total war. I looked back across Hiroshima, half-expecting another bomb to explode at any moment. I could only believe that this would be the beginning of World War III and the end of civilization as we knew it.

One of my first thoughts was of Doris and our son back in Abilene. I thought, *I'll never get back! The Air Force will recall me to active duty as a pilot, and I will be in Korea in just a few days!* My mind raced at full pitch, and all my plans seemed to change in the moment of that announcement.

I returned to Tokyo and began making arrangements to leave. Because of the war, all ships were full and passage seemed impossible. I finally located a Norwegian freighter that had space, and I knew that God was still guiding and taking care! He had given His protection and had used that summer to help prepare us for fifty years of missionary service. He was now returning me home for the final preparation.

We rejoiced over the salvation of 2,200 Japanese who had prayed to receive Christ as Lord, and gave thanks for the direction He gave to our ministry through those summer meetings.

EARLY YEARS AND PREPARATION FOR PARTNERSHIP

FOR OVER FIFTY-SEVEN YEARS we have been catching planes and trying to go where God leads in the ministry of world evangelism. The Lord prepared me for this as He built into me a great love for flying. By the time I was ten years old I was making models and studying airplanes day and night. In high school, I could name all our planes, both military and commercial, and identify their horsepower, type of engine, propeller, and speed. When an airplane flew over our house in the early 1940s, I would rush out the door and watch it until it passed out of sight. That love of flying, combined with World War II, would ultimately position me to be among the first pilots to enter Japan at the close of the war. It was there that He would give me a view and vision for world missions.

At fifteen, I took my first airplane ride in an open cockpit biplane, with two of my friends. We all three climbed into the front cockpit and were so crowded that we could not close the door or fasten the seat belt—a real thrill in the fog and

Chapter 4

low-hanging clouds. On my sixteenth birthday, Mother and Dad gave me a thirty-minute ride in a small Taylorcraft plane in Lubbock, Texas. That cost them two dollars, but no other gift could have been more appreciated. I was going to be a pilot!

Flying did become very important in our partnership campaigns. After my military days, a plane was provided for us to use in preparing for Partnership Evangelism. The airplane was always there, and it seemed I was always in it.

A God-Given Christian Home Life

A major factor in my preparation for Partnership Evangelism was the privilege I had of being raised in one of the greatest Christian homes in all the world. In this day of relaxed discipline and little spiritual training at home, I do not think I would have found God's plan for my life. God gave me what I needed. I don't think anyone ever had stronger discipline than we had in our family, and no one ever lived in an atmosphere of greater love and respect for their parents, contrary to the psychologists' opinions. Mother and Dad were a living testimony and expression of love and faith in God! William H. and Margaret Jackson provided the spiritual soil from which grew the vision for Partnership Evangelism and everything else He called us to do.

Inheriting a Vision for Missions

I learned the importance of missions very early. When I was just seven years of age, Mother and Dad were pastoring in Holiday, Texas, and preparing to make their annual missionary offering, called the Lottie Moon Christmas Offering. As always, they prayed and sought God's leading concerning what to give. To understand better the value of the gift they gave, we need to better understand their circumstances. They were in the midst of

With W. H. Jackson Sr. and Margaret Jackson

the Great Depression, and Dad's salary was only seventy-five
dollars a month.

Our parsonage was a four-room frame home with outside
facilities. (We used to call this "four rooms and a path.") The parsonage was located next to the church, and I remember well that
those were the days long before air-conditioning, paved roads,
ice, and phones. We didn't even have ceiling fans.

Money was in short supply, but we always seemed to have whatever was needed and never felt underprivileged. We had clean clothes, mostly handmade, and our house was spotless. There was one small lightbulb hanging in the middle of the room. This neatness was amazing since all windows and doors had to be left open for ventilation, and dust would filter in from the dirt roads.

Mother

It was to be a testimony to me of the kind of home God would want a Christian to have and was a part of the training God was giving to let me know that whatever we did for Him had to be the best!

Saturday was the day for cleaning and cooking in preparation for Sunday. I would have preferred playing to those cleaning chores, but even at age seven I found some joy in being a part of this great Sunday preparation. My chores were to dust, not only the top of the tables but the sides and underneath as well. Our nine-by-twelve linoleum rug— bought for twelve dollars— may have been worn, but it was polished. All things were put in order for the Lord's Day.

A job well done meant my sister and I could sit down and listen

Father

to Mother tell stories of miracles from the Bible. She would tell us how God's people, when faced with impossible tasks, would call on Him, and He invariably gave victory when all seemed to be impossible. What a lesson! I looked forward with great anticipation to these victory reports each Saturday morning. Instead of Saturday morning *Superman,* I had victory reports from God's Word. I learned that He still lived and was ready to provide the same victories today that He provided in the days of David, Daniel, and my parents. No doubt those days and those stories helped me refuse to accept any committee or denominational assignment that implied victory is not possible *now!*

That early training caused me to be expectant, then and now, and to know that God was able and would never let us down, regardless of the circumstances. How could we as Christians and victors ever approach our tasks with anything except joy and hope! How could we ever imply to a world that we might be faced with a situation where He was not adequate? If we should ever come to the place where circumstances should lead us to believe that God was not able, then we will have come to the place where we have finally proven Him to be inadequate and unfaithful in His promises to His people. That place and time will never come!

What Shall We Give?

In December 1931, Mother and Dad prayed and discussed what they could give to the Christmas offering. Mother asked Dad, "What do you think we ought to give?" He said, "I don't know, but we should make a *good* gift." Then he asked her what she thought of a twenty-five dollar contribution. Out of a seventy-five-dollar monthly salary, certainly that would be a major gift. Mother said, "I think we ought to give more." They prayed, and finally mother said, "I think we ought to give our entire December salary!" Dad said, "Let's pray about it." Dad was truly a man of prayer and was always sincerely seeking God's will in whatever they did. But I now wonder if, when faced with that particular challenge, Dad was just asking for time to delay the inevitable! One of the things in missionary life that has always been a burden to me has been our seeming willingness to delay in times of great need. We must always be on guard lest the statement "Let's pray about it" is used to delay making a decision we know the Lord would have us make *now*.

After much prayer, they agreed to give it all. I will ever be grateful for that decision, for in almost every valued activity I have been associated with, I have been called on to make what seemed to be unreasonable commitments in what appeared to be impossible situations! Mother and Dad made their commitment in spite of the temptation to be "reasonable" or "more realistic," for they understood it to be what God was asking them to do. The joys and victories recorded in this book have come about because God's people obeyed His leading to go and to do what seemed impossible, trusting God to give the victory.

When Mother and Dad made this decision, they immediately came to me and my sister and explained to us why they wanted to give all of their December salary to the missionary offering. They said that this would be used to tell boys and girls around the world about Jesus. They told us that this meant we would probably not be able to receive a Christmas present that year. As mother told us later, I hesitated at first but soon came joyfully saying I wanted to do this. I had wanted a drum for Christmas, but instead, God gave me a joy that is still with me today!

Miraculously, Mother and Dad had managed somehow to purchase a $1.98 basketball for me. And my grandmother, for the first time ever and without any knowledge of the Christmas offering, sent a doll as a gift for my sister Mary! It was a month of miracles and victory celebrations! We knew that we were participating in something that was letting the real Christmas story be told around the world, and we were excited and thrilled to have a part in it. God was already blessing.

More Miracles

Dad and Mother had not told anyone in the church about their decision to give all their December salary to missions, and they had explained to us that we might even be short of food. But I can still hear the horn on that Model A Ford as the farmer pulled up in front of our house and signaled his arrival! I rushed out the front door and across the porch to greet him as he sat waiting in the car with the motor still running. I jumped up on the running board, and he gave me a warm greeting as he handed me a big pan of homemade patty sausage. Dressed in his faded Big Ben overalls and a faded blue shirt, he said, "This is for your mother and dad. Would you take it to them?" I took the sausage and ran back across the porch calling, "Mother, look what God has given us!" I knew that God was taking care of us as He had promised. I was learning and would never forget that God keeps His promises, even in what may look like impossible situations!

Mother took the meat and broke the patties in half to make them go twice as far. Even keeping those patties in our new but primitive refrigerator, the meat spoiled! Mother prayed, "Lord, forgive me. I cut that meat in smaller patties just trying to make it go as far as possible. I know why it spoiled. It seemed to be good stewardship of God's gift, but I did that for fear there would be no more gifts! I will never do that again." Throughout the month God provided. This was a lesson I would remember twenty-five years later while sitting on the mission executive committee in Japan, discussing the financial needs for Japan evangelism. What missionaries and mission boards sometimes call a conservative use of funds is many times a demonstration of our fears and lack of faith in God to provide what is needed!

There is more! In that same December, some close friends of my parents came to Holiday for a visit. Mother wanted to invite them for a meal but had nothing to offer. Finally, she decided to invite them anyway, not knowing what she would serve. On the very day of the planned dinner, another member of the church, without any knowledge of my parents' needs or of their missionary gift, came bringing a dressed hen just in time for dinner. What a training ground for a missionary! He had provided again. We knew that God was providing. It told me again that we can depend on the Lord to provide when we follow and trust Him!

Through all of this we learned another valuable lesson. We learned that although we should be careful and not wasteful, sometimes things called "stewardship" and "conservation" are actually an expression of our lack of faith in God. I can remember talking to my dear friend, Pete Gillespie, a missionary in Japan, as we discussed what Southern Baptists could do to win Japan to Christ. Over and over as we would go to our executive committee and to the evangelism committees of both the mission and the Japan Baptist Convention, we would say, "God is able to provide whatever is necessary. What are we asking for?" We felt then, as I do now, that our responsibility was to find what was needed and to ask God for it. He would provide if we would ask, believing and knowing that He is *able*.

I have a firm conviction now, as I had at that time, that God's people will respond and will give whatever is needed if they know what is needed for a total victory. It is our job to ask for all that is needed in every task given to us! We usually ask for only what we

feel He may be able to provide, but rarely have we ever had sufficient faith to ask for all that is needed for the total victory. We
have been promised everything we need to win a major world-
witnessing victory. We must accept that as fact and ask for the victory! We have the challenge, the opportunity, and the resources
necessary to win whatever battle has been put before us. If we are
to see a world come to have the knowledge of Christ, we must
believe and "go in and possess the land." And I believe He means
now! He was able, He is able, and He will be able to give victory
now. Whether we are in the land of Japan, in the midst of
Buddhism, Shintoism, and materialism, or wherever we may be,
we have the message of hope and victory. "Ask and ye shall
receive!"

My father was a dynamic but unknown country preacher. He
had great love and humor and tremendous biblical messages. He
pastored small-town churches in Texas, but everywhere he and
my mother went, they set an example that I would always want
to follow. He was truly one of the great preachers of his day,
though few but God ever knew him!

His longest ministry was at Holiday, Texas, where he served
for seven years and saw over five hundred additions, 225 by profession of faith. He never stopped preaching. Mother passed away
at age eighty-six, and Dad served until he was ninety-seven, going
to Brazil on an evangelistic campaign at age ninety-four! In his
later years, rain or shine, he preached every Sunday in the Taylor
County jail and served as their chaplain well into his nineties.

Many servants of the Lord go into their ministries with the
promises of God as recorded in the Scripture as their guide. We
all have that opportunity, and it is more than enough encouragement for a Bible-believing servant of God. But in addition to those
recorded promises in God's Word, I had the privilege of seeing

scriptural promises confirmed and lived out daily in the life and work of my mother and father. Although they pastored only small churches in small towns and had neither a large salary nor funds from any inheritance, they ministered literally around the world. They lived in North Africa for a year, serving in a Christian orphanage, while living with my sister, Annette, and her husband Colonel Victor Lipsey, who was the air attaché for the U.S. embassy there. They served with us in Japan for more than two years and were a living testimony for all of us and to many of the young missionaries. On at least ten other occasions they participated in Partnership campaigns in as many countries around the world. They were always able to go and serve as long as they lived.

RETURN TO THE UNITED STATES— ASSIGNMENT JAPAN

IN EARLY JANUARY 1946, having completed my military service in Japan, I boarded the *U.S.S. Chanute Victory,* and we steamed out of Yokohama Harbor for Portland, Oregon, and home! After landing in Portland, we boarded a train for Fort Bliss, Texas, and the coveted discharge. From there I took a flight to the Midland-Odessa airport and the long-awaited and tearful reunion with my mother, father, and sisters. (Dad was pastor of the nearby Goldsmith Baptist Church.) Many times during World War II I had thought this day would never come!

I reflected on a day in primary flight training at Hatbox Field in Muskogee, Oklahoma, when I took my final check ride. My military and missionary career could have easily ended that day! My instructor and I were in an open cockpit Fairchild PT–19 and had just finished my flight exam. He was making notes and grading my flight, when suddenly from above, another cadet practicing spins came spinning down directly on us. I saw that the instructor making notes had not seen the plane, so I jerked the controls out of his hands and pulled left just in time to let the plane spin by us on our right side. The instructor took the

controls and chased the spinning plane to get his number!
Needless to say, he gave me high marks on that final check ride.
The Lord was with me then and until this special day, returning
to the United States and home!

My arrival was a clear answer to prayer, and I knew that God
had spared me for some purpose. This was a time of rededication
and of searching for His most perfect will. He had brought me
home with a vision and commitment for service that I would
never lose.

God Guides and Provides Life's Partner

Following my discharge in 1946, I enrolled at Hardin-
Simmons University in Abilene, Texas, to complete my college
work. God began leading me toward campaign evangelism by
inspiring me to begin a Youth for Christ program in Abilene.
At that time, YFC was a growing and vibrant organization that
had as its leaders men like Bob Pierce, Billy Graham, and Bob
Cook. Their commitment to evangelism was my inspiration and
example from the first campaign in Abilene until now. God also
led me to the greatest campaign associate I would ever know,

Dub   Doris

Doris Shirley. I was so impressed and inspired by her that it was only natural that in God's timing, I would ask her to marry me.

We did not receive much cooperation in setting up the youth rally, for at that time Southern Baptists and Texas Baptists did not support programs outside the denomination. Four years later, it was a shock to see and read of Texas Baptists' opposition even to Billy Graham, at that time a little-known evangelist.

As we sought to finance our youth rally, Texas Baptist leaders said that they had funds they could give to help us if we would change the name of the meeting to Baptist Youth Night. We explained that we were not trying to reach just Baptist young people but wanted to invite *all* young people into these services. I was not yet a volunteer for the ministry or for missionary service, but I felt the name Baptist Youth Night could keep some young people from coming.

A dedicated Baptist layman in Abilene, Doc Mead of the Mead Bakeries, said, "Dub, if you have any need financially for these rallies, just let me know! I will be glad to support it myself." I thanked him and told him that we could not let him carry the full burden for a rally that was for the whole city. It would have to be a responsibility of the entire city. Doc did contribute liberally to help us get started.

During World War II, I had saved practically all of my pay while in New Guinea and the Philippines. (After all, one can buy just so many coconuts in the jungles of the Pacific!) I had over three thousand dollars in savings, and my thought was to make that three thousand dollars last as long as possible! It was a joy to use those funds to help support the rallies.

I purchased a quarter-page ad in the *Abilene Reporter-News* to advertise the rally and rented an old Army BT–13 training plane to drop the advertisements, inviting all to attend that night.

Another ex-Air Force pilot went with me to throw them out as I flew. We took off and began throwing out the leaflets, concentrating on the high school seniors assembled at Hardin-Simmons. The Cowboy Band and Hardin-Simmons University Quartet were performing in the stadium just as we flew over.

The BT–13 is the loudest aircraft of the propeller age! It makes as much noise as a B–17 bomber over Berlin! I dove the plane toward the north goalpost, where the program was in progress, and went as low as I dared. We thundered across the field while my friend in the rear feverishly threw out the handbills. Later Doris told me that she cringed in the stadium as we flew through for fear someone would know that she was associated with that noise. She said the University Quartet, with my dear friend John Petry as soloist, was in the midst of one of their numbers, and the audience could not hear a word—just see their mouths moving!

I am not sure if it was the newspaper advertising or the leaflets we dropped, but we did have a large crowd and a great rally that night. God blessed that rally in many ways. It was a good start.

From the beginning, Doris was a constant encouragement. In difficult times, she never showed any discouragement. Those days and those battles were great times of preparation for the battles that would come in missionary work. We had worked together for about one year when the Lord made clear to us that we were to be married and serve together for life. I am eternally grateful that the Lord led me to Doris, a most faithful, loving, and patient partner. Had she been of the nervous, anxious, or critical type, we could never have experienced any of the victories that God has given in our fifty-five years of joyous service together.

Before marriage, we had discussed the possibility of mission service, for we knew even then that the Lord might be leading in that direction. We quizzed each other about our health and whether we knew of any problem that could keep us from serving overseas. If service overseas demanded a body that was strong, then that strong and healthy body would have been one of the evidences of God's leading.

A Physical Barrier to Mission Service

A traumatic and difficult time on our road to appointment as missionaries occurred when, after we were married and were almost ready for appointment as missionaries with the Foreign Mission Board, one of the doctors reported that Doris had a back problem that would make it impossible for her to serve overseas. We could not imagine that after all of these days and years of prayer and preparation and the deep conviction that the Lord had given to us concerning missionary service, we would now be unable to go because of health. It was a frustrating and confusing time in our search for God's will.

More than fifty years later, I learned that alone, and on our back porch, Doris had knelt and prayed, saying, "God, you have prepared Dub all his life for foreign mission service, and because of my bad back, I am keeping him from going. Lord, I would rather you just take my life than let me be the one to keep him from serving overseas." It is no wonder that the Lord used someone with a commitment like that to help keep the fires of witnessing alive until Partnership Evangelism became accepted as the tool that is letting the total church share their love for Jesus.

We sought a second opinion from a back specialist in Dallas, who examined her and said, "I have a bald head, and you have a bad back. We will always have these problems, but that should not hinder either of us too much." I said, quickly, "Will you put that in writing?" He gave us his report, and we forwarded it immediately to the Foreign Mission Board and received the final papers inviting us to Richmond, Virginia, for the appointment services in April 1951. God had led and was still leading.

God Leads Us All to Japan

Following graduation from Hardin-Simmons, I enrolled in Southwestern Baptist Theological Seminary to prepare for our return to Japan. I graduated in 1951 and in early August of that same year we boarded the *U.S.S. President Cleveland* in San Francisco and sailed for Japan, arriving on August 21. After long years of preparation, we were finally ready to begin sharing the joyous message of hope and salvation in a nation that had been waiting for so many years.

The two weeks on the *President Cleveland* were joyous times spent with my Doris, our three-year-old Bill, and our two-month-old Shirley. It was also a time of great anticipation as we realized we would soon be in Japan and able to share the message God had laid on our hearts. Those two weeks aboard ship also gave us time to become better acquainted with some of our fellow missionaries.

As the ship pulled into Yokohama harbor, I looked down from the deck and watched the men tugging on the ropes as they pulled us ever closer to our goal of sharing Christ in Japan. I could also see the little chapel on South Pier where we had enjoyed the many GI Gospel Hour services back in 1945. Across the pier in Yokohama I could see the crowds of Japanese, reminding me of those we had seen on the first day of the occupation when I landed my P–38 at Atsugi airfield in 1945. I was also reminded of the wonderful and effective crusades we had been a part of in 1950, working with Dave Morken and Youth for Christ.

I was sad that we had been so slow in getting back but glad we would soon be able to witness there again. We were eager to begin sharing with them the good news of what Christ had done for them and was willing to do now. As the ship docked and we were released to go ashore, I felt a strong impression that God was going to do something wonderful in Japan and that we could be a part of it. We knew Christ had given us the answer for every need these people might have, and we were being given the wonderful opportunity of introducing them to Him.

Our first two years of language school in Japan were among the hardest years of my life. But during those years it was a great joy to attend the Oimachi Baptist Church, where I had the privilege of working with Pastor Kenji Otani, one of the great preachers of Japan. It was always with joy and expectation that I boarded the train every Sunday and headed for Oimachi Church. On one bright Sunday morning, when I boarded the crowded train with my *Thompson Chain Reference Bible* under my arm, every seat on the train was filled, so I reached up and held on to a strap. I found myself standing in front of a Japanese young man who, by west Texas standards, looked like a hoodlum with his black leather jacket and a mean look on his unshaven face.

The young man stared at me as though transfixed, and I was concerned, for it was not normal for a Japanese to stare like that. He looked as if he thought I was the one who had dropped the atomic bomb on Hiroshima. Just as his gaze increased in intensity, he stood up right in my face and I thought, "Well, here it comes!" Surprisingly, in his halting English, he said, "Would you like to have my seat?"

I was absolutely astonished! I thanked the young man and was reminded that we cannot know what a person from another culture is thinking by using the standards we normally use to understand our people here at home. It is not possible.

Years later I would share this story in giving orientation to every one of our partnership participants, whether they were going to Sri Lanka, Germany, Spain, Italy, or wherever they might be going! This understanding and attitude is a must as we work with people from other cultures. I have always been grateful for the lesson God taught me through the action of that young man on the train that Sunday morning. We are just not qualified to judge a person in another culture.

My commitment was severely tested as we entered language school, for it was a challenging and difficult assignment. Nevertheless, I was determined to preach in Japanese, no matter how difficult it might be. Nothing was going to keep me from witnessing to the Japanese in their language.

With the passing of time and as I progressed in the language, I came to love preaching in Japanese even more than in English. I was never perfect, but I knew exactly what I was saying, even if the Japanese were sometimes confused! I have heard them say, "We did not always know exactly what you were saying, but we knew you loved us, and we got the message!" The motivation was much stronger in a Japanese setting, for most of the time I could be sure that most people in the audience were hearing the story of Christ for the first time. Although not perfect in the language, I learned enough of it to preach with real freedom and without notes!

Being able to speak directly to the people in their language was a *must*. Even now, these many years later, when I travel to Japan and have opportunity to preach, I enjoy preaching in

Japanese and can sense the Lord's presence and power in a very special way.

I recall one time in my frustration with the language that I told Cal Guy, my missions professor at Southwestern, that I could now preach on hell from experience!

Language study was important, but without question it was and is a mistake to put language ability above one's spiritual condition. I am sure members of the Japan Baptist Mission had an appreciation for the spiritual, but they rarely expressed their concern for such. To be fair, I assume they felt one's spiritual condition could be taken for granted. However, the only written requirement I can remember seeing concerned a missionary's accomplishments related to language ability. That was a mistake. All of us have been in meetings here at home where language was no problem, yet there was no evidence of God's power and presence and no results.

Mastering the language is important, and a missionary who is not in love with his task enough to try to learn the language will have a difficult time in ministry. The value of one's ministry, however, will be determined more by the obvious presence of Christ in the life of the missionary than in his language or in any other of his special abilities. We must realize that the individual's relationship with God and the presence of the Holy Spirit in his life is more important than any God-given talent he may possess.

I am sure that every missionary, mission executive, and pastor would say amen to this; but as we search for personnel to witness overseas, we need to make sure we place our emphasis on *spiritual* qualifications above everything else.

ASSIGNMENT ASAHIGAWA

WE MOVED FROM TOKYO and the Japanese language school in August 1953 and were more than ready to begin doing the work we had come to Japan to do! Our first choice for a place to serve had been the city of Hakodate, on the northern island of Hokkaido, for we had visited there and were impressed with the people and the challenge it seemed to present.

I have always believed that a person must follow his own God-given convictions concerning his life's work. However, in our case, the Japan Baptist Convention and Mission had decided that the next missionary assignment would be to Asahigawa, and we were the next missionaries. An impersonal decision like that was hard to accept, but after much prayer we decided that if we were to serve in Japan, we needed to cooperate.

We would move with our five children to Asahigawa, a city just a few miles away from the Russian-held Kurile Islands. The trip would take more than twenty-four hours by express train and ferry across the Tsugaru Straits from Honshu to Hokkaido, but we were getting closer and closer to the place where the Lord was going to give us one of our greatest joys and victories. We were ready!

Chapter 6

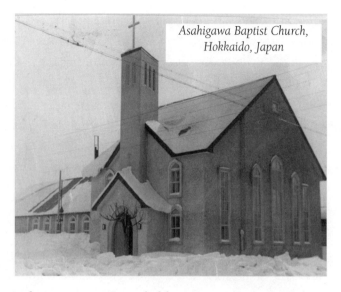

Asahigawa Baptist Church,
Hokkaido, Japan

Asahigawa is a city nestled between mountains in the center of the northern island of Hokkaido and was considered to be the coldest place in all Japan. The temperature often dipped down to 20 or 30 degrees below zero Fahrenheit in the winter, with snow six feet deep on the ground for four or five months of the year. It is also one of the hottest places in Japan during the summer because the mountains that surround the city block any breeze from the ocean.

It was, however, a place of friendly and open-minded people who had a progressive attitude that made it a fertile field for the gospel.

When we accepted this assignment, we knew there was no church and no members, only a challenge—a challenge to build a New Testament church in a city of 175,000 people! Asahigawa had been the Japanese military headquarters for the northern island of Hokkaido during World War II and was a very restricted area for religious activities. Nevertheless, we were confident that

God was leading and were determined to have a citywide presentation of the gospel. Matthew 5:16 was to be our guiding principle in all that we would do: Let your light shine in such a way in Asahigawa that all could see and understand.

Having no property, no church building, no adequate budget, and no church members, we needed to find the best possible meeting hall and use the best methods of presenting the message in order to see the Lord perform miracles if we were going to experience the victory that God only could give. We decided to begin by asking for the city auditorium. We learned from a Lutheran missionary in the city that a well-known Methodist missionary and evangelist, E. Stanley Jones, had just made a request for the auditorium and had been told it was impossible, because there was a city ordinance prohibiting the use of the building for religious purposes.

Since the city had refused Dr. Jones only a few weeks before, there appeared to be little hope of our receiving permission. But I had come to believe that we should never accept no until we had asked! I remembered that Matthew 7:7–11 says, "Ask and you shall receive," and Matthew 5:16 says, "Let your light shine in such a way that all will be attracted." With those verses and promises in mind, we prepared to meet with the city leaders and make the request.

At that particular time, Doris and I, together with my mother, preacher father, and younger sister, who were visiting with us, were praying earnestly for this campaign. On the day of decision, Doris and my father drove with me to the auditorium to make the request. We prayed for the Lord's guidance and remembered that several other pastors and churches in the States had also been asked to pray. I parked in front of the auditorium and went in to the business office where I was greeted by the short, stocky Japanese gentleman in charge. I explained to him that we were planning to make a presentation of the Christian faith to the people of Asahigawa and wanted to do it in the most attractive and effective way possible. I told him we had assembled the finest evangelistic team in Japan and knew that the best location for the meeting was his auditorium. When the manager opened a big schedule book, I thought, *Here comes the explanation that they do not permit religious activities in the auditorium.* However, as he studied the schedule, he said, "Those dates are open."

I thought, *How can he tell me the dates are open and then turn me down without losing face?* Then the big shock came! He said, "For a meeting like you have proposed, I will be glad to let you have the auditorium at half price!"

I realize that as you read this, at best, it can only be just an interesting story, but for this young missionary standing there in that empty auditorium, it was one of the most inspirational moments of my life. I had just watched the Lord turn water into wine again! He had answered prayer and performed another miracle! I was ready to shout!

I thanked the manager and struggled to restrain the joy and enthusiasm that made me feel like I could walk out of there without touching the ground and shout without saying a word.

What a lesson I had learned that day! Circumstances had said no, but God had said yes. We had asked the Lord for the best, and He had heard and answered our prayers.

I want to point out that I had not asked what it would cost. I knew that we had to have the auditorium and had asked to rent it, whatever the price. That is very important when we call on the Lord. We were following a God-given conviction that we should give Him our best and be willing to do or pay whatever it takes, regardless of the cost. If our program or plan is not worthy of asking for and expecting the best, we probably would not have found the plan God would have us use.

Southern Baptists, through our mission, an organization of all our Baptist missionaries in Japan, provided adequate funds for our home, church building, and even for our car. However the monthly fund for evangelism was only four thousand yen— U.S.$12.00, dollars or about U.S.$144.00 a year! Of course, it would not be possible to have an aggressive presentation of the Christian message in a city of 175,000 people using only those funds. We would have to launch out on faith and trust the Lord to provide whatever was needed.

During our one year in the nearby city of Sapporo, we commuted, prayed, and planned for the crusade to open the Asahigawa church. During that time we made detailed plans and prepared for the campaign that would introduce the Christian message and our church to the city. We determined that the first presentation of the gospel in that city would be made in the most attractive manner possible. Thus we did not start any kind of ministry until we were ready to make the all-out effort. To begin with anything less than our best would have given them the impression that our message was not urgent or important.

During the preparation visits we began to talk with the city leaders and even scheduled a banquet for them in the New Hokkai Hotel, the city's finest. The purpose of the banquet was to be up-front and explain to them why we were coming to Asahigawa. The chief of police, the president of the city's largest bank, and several other city leaders came to hear firsthand just what our purpose and plan were. Their response was positive, and they assured us of their wholehearted cooperation. The

Asahigawa Baptist Church was now formally introduced, even before the first meeting was held.

We purchased newspaper ads, printed the most beautiful handbills possible, and prepared attractive billboards to be strategically placed throughout the city. In addition, we printed 45,000 advertising sheets to insert in the newspaper the day before the meeting was to begin. The city also permitted us to use their loudspeaker system, installed up and down the major thoroughfares, to announce the meeting.

We purchased and used hot-air balloons and placed banners across the main street to advertise the crusade. One indication of God's continued presence and stamp of approval on this all-out effort was the miracle that took place on the day we asked the city for permission to put a banner across the main intersection. A city ordinance prohibited such banners. We met with the police chief, who had been one of our special guests at our introductory banquet and explained the purpose of the banner. He immediately assigned two policemen and sent them with their motorcycle and sidecar to help us hang the banner. What a joy and thrill to watch the Lord work!

Since we had no church members, we had hired day laborers to help pass out thousands of handbills and put up posters. We even hired a man with clown makeup and a sandwich board over his back to walk up and down the sidewalks in the center of town, banging a drum and ringing his tambourine to get attention and announce the campaign!

I will never forget the shock on the face of Pastor Otani, our key preacher, when he looked out of his hotel window and saw a caricature of himself painted on that clown's advertising board! We used every possible tool we could find to pass the message on to the people. Of course, television was not yet in use in Japan.

The campaign cost, including publicity, banquets, and other preparation, far exceeded the funds the mission had available for such a meeting. This kind of campaign had not been done before. Doris and I had decided that we would pay whatever was not covered by the mission. We were committed, whatever the cost!

Frank Connely, a blessed old China missionary who had been asked to come to Japan to serve as the treasurer of the mission, responded to my request for funds by saying, "Dub, we have many missionaries in Japan, and we cannot give you all of the funds at the expense of the others, but we will be in prayer about it."

I understood this, and we agreed we would just pray and move on! The mission's executive committee reviewed our request and, after prayer, provided one thousand dollars for the campaign, and we joyfully paid the difference.

I have always been glad that we did not make our decision concerning the kind of campaign we would have based on the limited finances that were available when we began. Had we made our plans on that basis, we would not have had the campaign. Our responsibility was to pray, plan, and commit to do what God was leading us to do, and then trust the Lord to provide. He did, and He does. He is always dependable!

The campaign team arrived, and our campaign opened on a Monday night with only sixty people present in that big auditorium. Nevertheless, because of the assurance we had in our hearts that God was leading and that we had done absolutely everything we could possibly do in preparation, we were not discouraged. There had been too many miracles to have any room for doubts now.

Tuesday night there were 120 present, and by Wednesday night the auditorium was packed, and people were standing around the walls!

During the week more than 350 people from Buddhist and Shinto backgrounds came forward, saying they wanted to receive Christ as Lord and Savior. This was truly a God-given victory and a wonderful beginning for a new church!

Saito San was one who came to know the Lord during the campaign. He had been walking by the auditorium when he was given an invitation to come in and hear the music and message.

Later he told us this story. He was crippled and, at the time of the meeting, had been drinking, although he was not drunk. He came in and sat down toward the back of the auditorium. His hat was still on, and he continued smoking his cigarette. Even though it was the first time he had ever heard the gospel, the Holy Spirit convinced him of the truth of the message, and he raised his hand during the invitation, saying he was accepting Christ as Lord! If I had reported that this young man who had never been in a church service before, never sung a hymn, and never heard the gospel until that night, had raised his hand saying he was receiving Christ as Lord, many would have had doubts that the decision was real.

Now, let me tell you the rest of the story! He joined our church, was baptized, and became a faithful church member, later surrendering to preach and graduating from our Baptist seminary. He went on to serve as pastor of the Obihiro Baptist Church on Hokkaido for over forty years, becoming one of the leading pastors on the island.

As I was writing the above testimony, I received an E-mail saying that he had just passed away and that they were having his

Our first baptismal service in Asahigawa

funeral that day! I am glad we did not have doubts about his salvation when he raised his hand and invited Christ to come in!

When someone tells me it is hopeless to expect anyone to receive Christ after hearing the message for the first time, I am not at all impressed, for I remember the promises in God's Word and remember Saito San and the many others who had come to know our Lord after hearing just one message and praying one simple prayer of faith! I am discouraged when I hear God's people say that cannot happen! Sometimes they say we must first develop a relationship, love, and teach them until finally they are able to know enough to accept Christ. Such thinking means salvation would depend on *our* personality and on *our* ability rather than on our Lord and a simple prayer of faith on the part of the one seeking to receive Christ. That kind of thinking is absolutely false and against everything the Lord has ever said concerning the plan of salvation! Some churches and even missionary organizations have difficulty accepting the fact that a person can receive Christ with just a simple prayer of faith. Salvation is the result of what our Lord does in answer to a prayer of faith, asking God for forgiveness through Christ and for the salvation He has promised. I myself became a Christian when I was only six years old. It was on a Sunday night in Holiday, Texas, as my father was preaching. Even at that young age, I was absolutely sure God had heard and answered my prayer.

The Asahigawa evangelistic crusade was one of the greatest and most inspirational weeks Doris and I have ever known. It was the blessed beginning of a New Testament church, and it taught us that the same message and power we had loved and shared back home in the United States would be just as effective in Japan or anywhere else in the world. We were not aware of it at that time, but it was also the beginning of Partnership Evangelism. There were eleven on that first partnership team, which included the two laymen, missionaries, musicians, and pastors.

Another miracle of this campaign must be reported here. God had given us Asahigawa's best auditorium for our campaign, but we had not been able to find a place for our church to meet. More than 350 persons had made decisions, and we were not able to tell them where our services would be held the next Sunday. Our entire team went to prayer again in our hotel room on Friday before the campaign was to close. We earnestly called on the Lord to lead us to our meeting place. We had been searching diligently every day but had not had any encouragement. While we were praying, a phone call came from Mr. Nonaka, president of the Takushoku Bank in Asahigawa, a friend whom we had come to know in our days of preparation. He said that we were welcome to use the second floor of his bank building for the services! That ended our prayer meeting, except for a joyous prayer of thanksgiving. It was another victory in a miraculous and victorious week.

On the first Sunday morning after the campaign, fifty-five new converts met with us in that rented room on the second floor of the bank building for our first service. We had gone from no members to fifty-five members in one week in Buddhist Japan.

Kenji Majima, Japan's most able evangelistic musician, led the congregational music on that first Sunday morning, singing *Amazing Grace* with missionary evangelist Pete Gillespie accompanying on the accordion. There were many tears of joy as Pete played and sang and bathed his accordion with his own tears.

In just a year and four months from the time of the opening campaign, we had the privilege of baptizing 117 former Buddhists, now joyous Christians, into our new church!

What a thrill it was, Sunday after Sunday, to feel and experience the presence of our Lord in every service. The memory of the commitment, dedication, and joy of those new Christians in Asahigawa is clear in my mind to this day. That experience illustrates how God can come quickly into the life of a church and make a joyous and revolutionary change.

From the very first service we saw wonderful and miraculous results and rejoiced over baptizing large numbers into the fellowship. We baptized the first thirteen in a river running through Asahigawa just before the heavy snows began to fall. Even so, this baptism was marked by cold winds and rain that came during a typhoon that claimed the lives of fourteen hundred people in a ferry boat disaster in the straits between Honshu and Hokkaido.

Baptismal candidates, for lack of changing facilities, were forced to wear their wet clothing for over an hour after the service before we could get them to a place to change. That is, all but one. One of the young men resorted to a Japanese custom, not unusual in those days, of changing clothes in public, and did so there on the beach in full view of us all, as we closed by singing "O Happy Day!"

That incident, along with others, caused us to expedite our search for an acceptable place to baptize. Before we solved our problem, we had seven more ready to be baptized, and we were forced to use a Japanese bath house. The manager of the bath house said, "We will charge you one hundred *yen* per person." We explained to him that this was not actually a regular bath we were paying for and that, in fact, we did not want him to use hot water. He complied, and even though the weather outside was freezing, he gave us ice-cold water! As I baptized Sato San, a young high school student, the water was so cold that he stiffened just as I raised him out of the water and his head hit the plumbing, literally shaking the little Japanese hotel.

The next baptismal service was on Christmas Day in 1955. To this day we remember that Christmas as the most joyous we have ever experienced. Nearly a hundred of the new church members met in our living room to celebrate their first Christmas as Christians. The menu that evening was Japanese *mikans,* or tangerines, and hot chocolate, but it was a feast unequalled before or since!

Following the singing and testimonies, we moved from the living room into the one-car garage for a special baptismal service. Snow was falling heavily outside, and since we had no baptistry, we purchased a wooden whiskey barrel that was eight feet in diameter, six feet deep, and scrubbed clean. We built stairs into and out of the barrel, and from that day to this we have sometimes jokingly said, "We believed in the preservation of the saints!" Mr. Ueno, a fifty-three-year-old carpenter, had built the steps and was one of those to be baptized. Ninety-two of us huddled around one kerosene stove in the privacy of that garage, and with the subzero temperatures outside, we gave thanks as we baptized thirteen more converts on the birthday of our Savior.

Our motto or goal, "Whatever It Takes," had served us well. Before the church building was finished, we had several others to baptize, so we rented another public bath house, and again the proprietor failed to follow what we thought were clear instructions. Contrary to our request, the manager filled the pool with the usual steaming, red-hot bath water. He wanted us to have the very best! After we sang a hymn, I gritted my teeth and waded into the hot water. The Japanese candidates were accustomed to extremely hot baths. They made it just fine, but I had some trouble. The steam made it almost impossible for the members to observe the baptismal service. They literally had to take their cues for singing from the sound of the water as I baptized. They couldn't see. After we finished, the confused proprietor was hesitant to take our money, noting that we had entered the pool fully dressed.

When we dedicated the beautiful new Asahigawa Baptist Church building, we were grateful for an inside baptistry. During one of the first services in the new building, I had the privilege of baptizing Mr. Nagayama and his wife. They later became two faithful church members, and Mrs. Nagayama served as president of the women's organization for many years. Mr. Nagayama was nervous and excited about being baptized. When I spoke to him I noticed a strong odor of alcohol and thought to myself, *What would Texas Baptists say if they knew I was about to baptize a man who had just had a pretty strong drink to get him through the service!* Quickly I went through the Scriptures in my mind as fast as I could, and I did not immediately recall one that said not to baptize him. Remembering the time of his decision, I was certain he had accepted Christ and was in line for believer's baptism. He was young in the Lord and not yet knowledgeable of all the ways God would have him live. We were not there to baptize perfect people but to baptize those who wanted to start their new Christian life in obedience to the Lord in baptism. Thus in the security of our little church, eight thousand miles away from home, I baptized him and vowed to teach him the ways God would have him live. Later I was able to share with him the dangers of alcohol and the joys of being obedient to our Lord in Christian living.

Amazing Christians

I cannot leave the story of this new church without telling about two of the most amazing and dedicated Christians Doris and I have ever known. Two of those members especially illustrate the faithfulness and tremendous spirit God gave to those new Christians.

Mr. Ishizaka was one of the first men to make a decision for Christ in our opening campaign. He was forty-four years old and a man with a responsible position in a coal mining company. He had a special joy and enthusiasm in his newfound faith! He diligently studied the Scriptures and grew daily in his faith.

Before the new church building was completed, I continued to commute from Sapporo to Asahigawa, a three-hour train ride, and stayed in the New Hokkai Hotel over Saturday and Sunday of each week.

I tacked a sign-up sheet on the outside of my hotel room door and invited the members to sign up for study and discussion periods every Saturday. Each week the schedule would be full, and it was amazing to see those new Christians coming to ask questions and study their Bible. Mr. Ishizaka seemed to have more questions than any of the other members. His Bible was already well marked from his long hours of study.

In the Sunday and Wednesday night services, he usually stood at the front door of the church to hand out songbooks and Bibles and welcome the members and visitors as they arrived.

After about a year of faithful service, he came to me and said, "I am sorry, but my company is transferring me to another city. I am to supervise the building of a railroad in a coal mine." My heart sank. How could we lose such a faithful member? I gave him a word of encouragement and said, "Perhaps God intends for you to start a new church in that city." Nevertheless, the next Sunday morning, to my great surprise, he was present, standing in his usual place handing out songbooks and Bibles with the same joyous smile and confident Christian expression on his face. I could hardly wait to close the service and ask him what had happened. "Mr. Ishizaka, I thought you were not going to be here this morning." "I prayed about it," he said. "The greatest thing that ever happened to me was coming to know Christ as Savior, and I cannot leave my church. I resigned my job. Nothing is more important to me than this church." That was typical of the kind of commitment those new Christians had!

Mrs. Tabogami, a new convert, was another illustration of total commitment. She radiated the joy I believe God wants every Christian to have. Her first visit to our church was on a Sunday morning when she came wearing a black kimono and an expression of gloom and grief as dark as her kimono. I was teaching the women's Bible class on the second floor of the church when she entered. She pushed open the sliding door of our classroom and, kneeling, she slid across the *tatami* floor and took her place with bowed head.

She was only in her forties, but because of the burden and grief she was carrying, she appeared to be much older. Later we learned that she had come because of seeing the great change in the life of her teenage son, who had accepted Christ a few weeks earlier. Only one week after his conversion, as he was riding his bicycle down the street through the deep snow and icy ruts, he was struck by a truck and killed.

His mother had been very impressed by the tremendous change in his life, even in that one week following his conversion. She decided to find out what had made the difference. She said that before his conversion, her son was very introverted and had even shown some suicidal tendencies. There had been no evidence of joy in his life. But after his conversion he had become a young man filled with joy and hope! She knew that what he had found in his Christian faith was something she needed in her hour of sorrow.

Following the Bible class, Reverend Shibata, who had just come to serve as the new pastor, brought the morning message and, as was the custom in our church, gave an invitation at the close of the service. Although this was the first Christian service Mrs. Tabogami had ever attended, she came forward and joyously asked the Lord to give her forgiveness, salvation, and eternal life.

After her salvation experience she became the most joyous and radiant Christian we had ever seen. She appointed herself as the official church greeter. She would greet the people with her smile as they came in, hand them a pillow (*zabuton*) to sit on in the cold church building, and then offer them some hot tea that she always had brewing on top of the coal stove.

During those days I invited Bob Culpepper, a professor at Seinan Gakuin Seminary in Fukuoka, to come and help teach the cardinal doctrines of our Baptist faith. Naturally one of our meetings covered the teaching of stewardship and the scriptural plan of giving. Following that service she asked if she could talk to us concerning tithing. She explained how glad she was to hear that message, for ever since becoming a Christian, three months earlier, she had given her entire month's salary in the offerings and had been living on water, rice, and dried salt fish in order to give everything to the Lord who had given everything to her! This she had been doing in great joy!

Doris and I have often said that she radiated the greatest joy of any person we have ever known. She looked on giving as a joyous opportunity. It was no wonder that the little church became self-supporting in just over one year and was the first church in the Japan Baptist Convention to call a full-time music minister and pastor in that brief time!

When the little church voted to call the music minister, they demonstrated unusual boldness and great faith by asking Mr. Kenji Majima of Tokyo to move with his family to Asahigawa, a city that was 750 miles north of his home in Tokyo. The church also voted to pay their moving expenses and a salary that was in line with what the secular world paid. They did not take note of the fact that even the largest Baptist church in Japan did not have a full-time music director. They just saw a need and trusted God to meet it. In that same Sunday afternoon business meeting, they also voted to declare the church self-supporting! That business session following the morning service, with testimonies and the revival spirit that permeated it, lasted until 2:30 P.M.

One non-Christian grandmother who had been present stood and said, "Although I am not a Christian, I would like for you to know that as I come to church, I will bring the wood on my back to be used for heating the home of this new music director!" She kept her promise and every Sunday morning walked across a mountain carrying the wood to church.

One young member, who had just recently entered military service, pledged to buy a slide projector for the church. It would take him more than a year to meet his pledge, for he was a private in the Japanese army.

Mr. Ishizaka gave their family heirloom, a three-string *samisen* musical instrument, and Pastor Shibata took off his watch and a valuable ring and laid them on the altar. I think I can say that everyone present gave all they could give! Rarely can that be said about any stewardship effort anywhere in the world. We watched this congregation give and do whatever it took to build a great church in the name of Christ in their city. The Asahigawa experience convinced us that this same exciting and enthusiastic evangelistic ministry could and should be repeated in every city in Japan! It marked the beginning of our thinking about a similar campaign for the city of Tokyo! Later that would be called the New Life Movement and Partnership Evangelism. Partnership would eventually become a blessed part of our International Mission Board's plan to reach a world for Christ.

In January 1983, twenty-eight years after leaving Asahigawa, Doris and I had the privilege of returning to preach a morning service. When we entered the church, the first person we met was Mr. Ueno, the carpenter, who had turned the whiskey barrel into a baptistry. We were thrilled to see him, and he reminded us that I had been the one who had shared the plan of salvation with him. "It is just like a dream that you are here again." It was certainly a dream come true for us. We watched him as he went through his usual ritual of taking his place on the second row, placing his Bible and hymnal on the little pulpitlike stand he had fashioned to fit over the back of the pew in front of him, turn up his hearing aid, and look with anticipation to me for the message he had come to hear. It was like old times. Even at age eighty-two, Mr. Ueno had traveled twenty minutes by train and walked over a mile through the snow to be there.

Many others present that morning had been in that memorable first Christmas service so many years ago—now Sunday school teachers and faithful leaders of the church. There was Mr. Watanabe, the druggist, and his brother, a dedicated farmer; Mrs. Nagayama, now the president of the women's organization and her husband, who though very ill with a heart ailment, had insisted that they bring him from the hospital in his wheelchair. When the invitation was given, he asked his wife to push him to the front in order for him to publicly rededicate his life to the Lord. It was another great hour of inspiration and decision and another evidence of God's continued blessings on those faithful people! Remember, Mr. Nagayama was the man I had baptized with the smell of whiskey on his breath!

Doris and I continue to thank the Lord for letting us be a part of that church, one of the best churches we have ever seen, one where most of the members had become Christians immediately after hearing of the gospel message for the first time. All of those members had left Buddhism and Shintoism to become shining examples of what a Christian can and should be. This is another testimony of the love and power of our Lord!

Another Life-Preserving Miracle

While in Hokkaido, I chose to remain in the Air Force Reserve and traveled by military courier to Tokyo every month or two for training.

On one of the trips to Tokyo, after finishing my flight training session, I attended a missionary meeting in the home of Edwin and Mary Ellen Dozier. I had decided that rather than take the military flight back home, I would ride the train with some of our missionary friends. I wanted to enjoy some of the good fellowship with those returning by train.

On the way to the train station I was asked to drive one of our missionaries back to her home. As I drove toward the mission compound, I found myself in one of the worst traffic jams I have ever been in. Six lanes of traffic were standing still! I realized that this traffic could cause me to miss the train and force me to return home on the military flight after all.

I pulled out of the stalled line of traffic and made a new line right down into the center of the jam. Immediately I could see that a stalled bus was the problem. I got out of my car and boarded the bus, asking all the passengers to get off and help me push the bus out of the way. I tried to tell the nervous and sweating driver to "put it in neutral and we will push!" However, I had a struggle, for I could not remember any phrase in my Japanese language book that said, "Put it in neutral!" Somehow I got the message across, and we pushed the bus to one side and released the traffic.

The grateful policeman was overjoyed, and I was shocked when he held up his hand and stopped all traffic again. He then pointed his finger toward me and motioned for me to move forward as he held all the traffic until I was completely free and on my way to the train station. It was his way of saying thank you, and as I realized later, it was the Lord's way of sparing my life for the joyous work ahead.

The policeman's kindness toward me made it possible for me to make my train and ride home with my missionary friends. About twenty-four hours later, when I arrived back in Hokkaido, I heard on the Armed Forces Radio station that the Air Force courier plane, a C–46 transport that I had been scheduled to fly on, had crashed into the straits between Honshu and Hokkaido and all the passengers had been killed.

Doris and my mother were shopping that afternoon when they heard the report of the crash. Doris knew that I had planned to take that flight home, so there was great relief and thanksgiving when I called and told her I had come home by train.

TOKYO BAPTIST CHURCH

IF YOU HAVE EVER BEEN ASKED to do something you did not want to do, you will be interested to see how God can take such a situation and turn it into a great victory and joy. God gave us a victory in just such a situation, in Tokyo back in 1957.

When we returned to Japan after our furlough in 1957, the personnel committee of the Japan Baptist Mission asked us to consider starting what was to be the first English-language Baptist church sponsored by Southern Baptists overseas. We had come to Japan to see Japanese come to know Christ. We had a wonderful experience in Asahigawa, and we really wanted to do it all over again. With this God-given burden for the Japanese, we found it hard to accept the idea of building and establishing a church so that Americans could have another option to hear the story of Christ, a message the Japanese had never heard!

At the time we could not understand what God was doing, but since we were available, we accepted the pastorate and responsibility of organizing and building Tokyo Baptist Church. We agreed to this assignment with the understanding that as soon as it was built, we would return to our Japanese work. Later we would recognize that this would be another major step toward seeing a citywide campaign for Tokyo and the beginning of the Asiawide New Life Movement, a movement that would be the most effective and far-reaching evangelistic effort we would ever have the privilege of being a part of. It would also be a big step toward setting up Partnership Evangelism.

We enthusiastically began working with the English-speaking community—businessmen, military personnel, and missionary families. We invited twenty-seven of the persons interested in starting this church to come to our home and pray with us as I explained to them the conditions under which we would consider being a part of such a project.

All those who attended that first meeting were told of our long-standing commitment toward winning Japan for Christ. I rarely write down in detail conditions on which I will accept a task, but this meeting was so important that I did so before accepting the challenge of building Tokyo Baptist Church. In essence, the paper pointed out that we had come to Japan praying that the Japanese might come to know and receive Christ as Lord. We knew that we could not depart from that God-given vision just to provide a ministry that would make it a little more convenient for Americans to have another opportunity to hear the gospel, while most Japanese had not yet heard for the first time.

I explained to those who came that our number-one priority would be winning Japan to Christ and building a church that would serve as an example for all Japan and Asia. We wanted to join with them in building such a church. I reminded them that such an effort would demand *total* commitment, not just our spare time and our tithe. We would not be interested in building another ordinary church with an ordinary vision, for we already had enough ordinary churches. We could not justify taking valuable time away from the Japanese ministry to establish a church

Groundbreaking at Tokyo Baptist Church

that might become a poor example and even a hindrance to the cause of Christ in that great land.

Everyone present was in total agreement! God had been present, and we were ready to go! Before closing, we also agreed that we would claim Matthew 7:7–11 and Matthew 5:16 as the guide for our every action: "Ask and ye shall receive," and "Let your light shine in such a way that when men see it they'll say 'that's for me.'" We were a small group, but we were committed to plan and build in a way that the goal our Lord had set before us when He said, "All things are possible" and that He was "not willing that any should perish," would forever be our goal and driving purpose. That goal demanded that in the building of our church we would have to have the very best possible location and facility for God's people in the world's largest city.

We had no money or budget to guide us as we drew up the plans for our new building, so we were unrestricted in our planning and could propose and build exactly what we felt the Lord would have us build. From the very beginning we determined to build so that all observers could easily see and understand the importance and the urgency of our message. We were free to seek God's will and then trust Him to provide for the vision He had given. We knew that we were setting out on a course that would require miracles and God's constant direction. In that very first meeting with the twenty-seven interested folk, we agreed to raise $50,000 within the next six months! With that agreement, we had prayer and went out to go to work. God had been present, and He had led. We knew from that first night that He was going to give us the church building and the ministry in Tokyo He wanted us to have.

Our first task was to find an acceptable meeting place. The little group of interested people was meeting in a borrowed military chapel. I was especially concerned and praying about this urgent need when I signed in for my annual two weeks of active duty with the Air Force at Haneda in Tokyo. I was committed to upgrade my training as an Air Force pilot each year, but I did not dream that God was going to use that to help provide our first building! After completing my duty, I reported to the commanding officer and, as usual, saluted and thanked him before leaving. He knew I was a missionary and asked, "Could you use any buildings?" I said, "Yes, we have an urgent need." He said, "I have five quonset huts that you can have at no charge if you can get them off the base in thirty days." Immediately I told him we would take them, wondering where I would put them, since we had no property! It was the beginning of a million miracles and of the many victories God was going to give!

The next day I set out in earnest with George Hays and Curtis Askew—two fellow missionaries—to search for property. I had already looked in many choice areas, but on this cold morning we drove to another beautiful and ideal area and began to search door to door. We came upon a choice piece of property, set off by three palm trees, on a beautiful thoroughfare. I had a strong feeling that this was where the Lord would have us build the church. When we inquired about the property we learned that it belonged to a Chinese banker who lived across the street, so the three of us went in to see him. We told him we were interested in buying the property, and he indicated that he would be willing to sell. Surprisingly he quoted us a price of $35,000, which was well within the market value. Without a penny available, we told him we would take it! I am so glad we started that way! Too many programs are started based upon our own vision and available resources rather than on what we believe God can and will do.

As we left the banker's home, I said, "By the way, I have some buildings I would like to put on the property while we are working out the details of the sale." "That will be fine," he said, and we knew God had performed another miracle, because in Japan, the law says that once you put a building on a piece of property the owner cannot evict you! Most landowners are careful to let no one put anything on their property until it has been paid for in full.

A few days later an American sergeant from Mississippi pulled up in a large military truck and unloaded the five Quonset huts onto the property that would soon become the first home of Tokyo Baptist Church. A beautiful but temporary building was made from the Quonset huts, and within weeks people began coming from all over Tokyo to our services. We were not people of wealth but a people with confidence in the Lord. We knew He was guiding, and from the beginning we assumed the responsibility for raising the $135,000 needed to build our temporary building and the permanent building, plus the $35,000 for the property. As I record this today, those figures do not seem to represent much of a challenge. But on a salary of about 160,000 yen (about $450 a month), it was impossible.

The funds started coming in. The Foreign Mission Board loaned us $25,000, and every member began giving sacrificially. Even family members back in the States contributed thousands of dollars to the building. From the beginning, we had told the little group that tithing alone would never be enough. It would require total commitment!

Giving Beyond Ability

As we pressed for the needed funds month by month, one of our women, Joan Steele, who had already given all she could, took a little piece of paper from the back of a Sunday school envelope and wrote, "John and I give our Buick convertible," and placed it in the offering plate. Judy Garrett, a schoolteacher in the military school system, after giving all that she had, borrowed money on her home in Florida in order to give! She, like the rest of us, was convinced that this church would make possible the salvation of many around the world. Major Schmidt, who served on our building committee, was a new Christian and in love with his Lord and the church. One evening he quietly handed me a check for $8,500 for the building. Remember this was 1957, and these were people without wealth!

Sergeant Charles Matthews was chosen as our first chairman of deacons, and Sergeant Trozy Barker was selected to serve as the first Training Union director. His wife, Emma Jean, became my first secretary. Major Leo and Arlene Bradford became faithful and dynamic leaders in the new church, traveling many miles back and forth every day from Johnson Air Force Base.

Mary Lee Askew and Helen Hayes, two Tokyo missionaries, were faithful teachers and leaders in the church, and Ernest and

Ida Nelle Hollaway, Theron and Juanita Farris, Frank and Wynon Gillham, and many other missionaries and dedicated Christians joined in prayer, fellowship, and service in order to see the church come into being.

Our permanent three-story steel-and-concrete building began to take shape! In less than two years, the Lord had given us our new building, which with a few

Tokyo Baptist Church

additions is still the home of Tokyo Baptist Church today. It was dedicated in November 1959 with only $25,000 still owed! God led, and He provided, and we had the joy of watching!

Joy in Ministry

The major tone of that new church was joy, joy, joy, work, work, work, and more joy! We saw many come to receive Christ as Lord and forty-four people make decisions for full-time Christian service in that brief year and a half. Eight of those were under appointment by the Foreign Mission Board by the time the church was two years old!

Mr. MacPherson, head of the American Red Cross in Tokyo, came to me one Sunday and said, "I am going to have to miss one of the next two Sundays. Which Sunday should I miss?" I was thrilled that the joy and excitement in the church was so great that one of our members hated to miss even one Sunday. *If our churches are what they ought to be, they will be filled with joyous people full of anticipation as to what the Lord is going to do, regardless of the battles they are in!*

The day we started Tokyo Baptist Church, we had agreed that the church's ministry was to reach all Japan and the world for Christ. Many times in our prayer meetings I can remember some-one praying, "Lord, let us be a part of city, nation, and world revival." I do not remember a prayer of "Lord, give *us* revival." God hears that kind of praying, and He always answers. That is why I wasn't surprised that seven years later, in Tokyo Baptist Church, more than five hundred Americans, most of them from Texas, knelt and prayed before fanning out across all Asia to witness. The result of that campaign was the salvation of more than 45,000 people from Japan to Singapore in just six weeks! How can one ever evaluate the ministry of a small church when their prayer is, "Lord, let us be a part of world revival." The wonderful and amazing fact is that any church, regardless of size, can have that goal and pray that prayer, and God will hear and answer.

Our goal to let our light shine for all Japan and the world to see was aided by our good relationship with the press in Japan. I had asked the *Japan Times,* the largest English-language newspaper in Japan, to provide a sixteen-page supplement for the dedication of the new church building. Masaru Ogawa, managing editor of the *Japan Times,* gave us four full pages in a Tokyo Baptist Church dedication supplement. On the front page of the paper, in bright red letters, it read, "Tokyo Baptist Church Dedication Edition!" On top of all of this, Richard Ostling, religion editor of *Time* magazine, ran a beautiful story on the beginning of Tokyo Baptist Church.

Advertising had covered most of the cost for the supplement, but Doris and I were left with a bill of $1,200 that had to be paid to the paper on the week of the dedication. Twelve hundred dollars to a Baptist missionary in 1959 was a lot of money, so I decided to sell my electric organ to make the final payment.

One morning during the dedication week, Billy Souther, longtime minister of music at the First Baptist Church of Dallas and our music director for the week, was sitting with me in the living room of our home reviewing the joys and victories God had been giving. As we talked, the doorbell rang, and a buyer for the organ came in with the needed twelve hundred dollars, just minutes before a representative of the *Times* rang the bell asking for the twelve-hundred-dollar balance we owed to them! Another blessed miracle!

In addition to the *Times,* the *Mainichi English Language Newspaper* and the *Asahi Evening News* cooperated and ran stories and pictures in preparation for the dedication. Praise the Lord, every English-speaking person in all of Tokyo—and there were thousands of them—had learned about our new church in that one week of dedication! God was answering the prayers of the people and giving blessings every day!

During our week of dedication, I am sure we had the greatest preaching, singing, and special music to be found anywhere in the world. We had done our best, and God had done the rest! He had given us the most beautiful church building in Japan and had let all the English-speaking population of the world's largest city know that the church was open and that they were welcome.

Participants in this dedication included some of America's most beloved spiritual leaders. Billy Souther of the First Baptist Church in Dallas led our choir. Our speakers were Ramsey Pollard, of Bellevue Baptist Church in Memphis, Tennessee, and president of the Southern Baptist Convention; T. A. Patterson, executive secretary of the Baptist General Convention of Texas; Herschel Hobbs, radio pastor for the *Baptist Hour* and also an SBC president; T. B. Maston, professor of Christian ethics at Southwestern Seminary; E. Hermond Westmoreland, pastor of

South Main Baptist Church in Houston, at that time the greatest missions-giving church in the convention; G. Kearney Keegan, beloved secretary of the department of student work in Nashville; and Jim Stertz of the Foreign Mission Board. We even had a youth rally that week, led by a young sixteen-year-old student preacher who later became president of the Southern Baptist Convention— Paige Patterson.

The Japan Philharmonic Orchestra and the Fifth Air Force Band provided music for the celebration. Paul Michelson of the Billy Graham organization; Kurt Kaiser, composer and vice president of Word Records; Paul Goercke, an outstanding pianist; and Ralph Carmichael, the undisputed leader in Christian musical arrangements, all provided their talents for the dedication week.

We heard messages of congratulations from many of Japan's leaders. Governor Ryotaro Azuma of the Tokyo Metropolitan Government said, "It is a matter for gratification that by the dedication of the Tokyo Baptist Church, another place of worship is given to the citizens of Tokyo, who justly enjoy freedom of religion. I sincerely look forward with much expectation to the future activities of this church and the promotion of the welfare of the citizens of Tokyo." Governor Azuma became our friend and later was helpful in our preparation for the New Life Movement and the Tokyo partnership.

Douglas MacArthur II, the American Ambassador to Japan, said, "The dedication of the Tokyo Baptist Church on November 1 should serve to remind all of us once again in this troubled world in which we live that human understanding and divine guidance are essential to the salvation of mankind. I offer my hearty congratulations to all who have contributed to making this church, where all may come to worship and gain divine inspiration, a beautiful and living reality."

Lieutenant General Robert Burns, commander of the United States forces in Japan, said, "I extend sincere thanks to all who have contributed time, effort, and money, to make possible this occasion. May this beautiful church structure symbolize all that is sacred in man's life and essential in our national life."

Ramsey Pollard said, "Personally and on behalf of Southern Baptists, I wish to bring greetings and congratulations for this eventful occasion in the life of your great church. It is my sincere judgment that the future of the church is as bright as the promises of God. Southern Baptists are proud of the work that has been done by your church."

Herschel Hobbs said, "When the apostle Paul wrote to the church in Philippi, he called them a little colony of heaven set down amid the earth's deep need. When he wrote to the church in Thessalonica, he called them a sounding board for the gospel. These two phrases describe the position of Tokyo Baptist Church perfectly. Here is a colony of heaven located in an area of the earth which desperately needs salvation. Grant, my Lord, that this church will ever be a sounding board for the gospel, that the good news might be known throughout all of Japan and the Orient."

Calvin Parker, chairman of the Japan Baptist Mission, wrote: "The mission heartily salutes a noble church. We are grateful to Dub Jackson and other missionaries who have been able to share their ministry with the church. We are confident that the Tokyo Baptist Church will continue to assist the mission and the convention while ministering effectively to the large English-speaking population of Tokyo and serving as a model church for all Japan."

Baker James Cauthen, the executive secretary of the Foreign Mission Board, said, "I congratulate you, the members of the Tokyo Baptist Church, for the organization and development of your church. This development in your great city will mean much in the furtherance of the Lord's work. We are watching your progress with interest and joy. May God's richest blessings be upon you."

Winston Crawley, the Foreign Mission Board's secretary for the Orient, said, "The Tokyo Baptist Church is one of the strongest of the English-language Baptist churches in the world's major cities. I am happy to express for the Foreign Mission Board greetings and congratulations with the assurance of our desire to continue in happy fellowship and cooperation. I am praying that the Lord will enlarge and bless this ministry in a remarkable way."

T. A. Patterson, executive secretary of the Baptist General Convention of Texas, said, "It is my earnest prayer that the Lord will be able to use us in some way to assist in the marvelous work which the members of this church have begun."

K. Owen White, pastor of First Baptist Church, Houston, and later president of the Southern Baptist Convention, said, "The organization of the English-speaking Tokyo Baptist Church is assuredly one of the greatest things that has happened in recent years. The church can serve missionaries, military personnel, educators, English-speaking civilian workers, and Japanese people. I believe this church is destined to hold a great place in the religious and social life of Tokyo. My personal contact with the Tokyo Baptist Church has filled me with enthusiasm for its future."

Masa Nakayama, a member of Prime Minister Ikeda's cabinet and the first woman ever to serve as a cabinet minister in Japan, spoke at the dedication on "My Christ and My Church." This godly woman was a great encouragement to all of us.

We were constantly amazed that in less than two years, God had given to us a beautiful new church building and one of the most victorious congregations we had ever seen. All of this when circumstances had said it was impossible!

Lest We Forget

General Minoru Genda was a brilliant strategist who helped plan the attack on Pearl Harbor. After the war, he served as commander of the Japanese Self-Defense Force and was a senator in the Japanese Diet until his recent death. In 1958, Major Galen Bradford, a pilot and later chairman of our deacons, said that when he invited General Genda to attend our church, the general said, "I don't understand you Christians. If we had won the war, we would have built a Buddhist temple on every high hill in America by now. If this Christianity is so important, why are you so slow?" He was right on both counts: they would have built those temples, and we were slow!

Highlights of TBC

Looking back on the two years at Tokyo Baptist Church, some of the highlights that come to mind are the organization of the church and the presentation of a challenge to be a part of world revival. Other highlights were the dedication of the new building and funding for Pastor Matsumura's trip to the Southern Baptist Convention meeting in Florida to invite Billy Graham to come as the main speaker for the New Life Movement Crusade. Tokyo Baptist Church had been a major step in seeing the New Life Movement and Partnership Evangelism become a reality.

I cannot help but remember my reluctance to accept the pastorate of an English-language church—but what a joy to see today how God used Tokyo Baptist Church to launch an Asia-wide evangelistic campaign in which 45,000 Asians prayed to receive Christ as Lord and Savior in just six weeks!

THE NEW LIFE MOVEMENT

EVERYTHING RECORDED UP UNTIL NOW has been a record of God's leading and preparation for the New Life Movement and Partnership Evangelism. The NLM was a massive evangelistic campaign in 1963 that grew from Tokyo to include all Asia! More than 45,000 people across Asia came out of Buddhism and Shintoism, saying they wanted to receive Christ as Lord and Savior in that campaign of just six weeks! The New Life Movement was the big step toward beginning Partnership Evangelism, in which ordinary, loving Christians come together to share their faith and invite those without Christ to receive Him and life eternal.

God Leads in the Japan Baptist Mission Meeting in 1957

A major event in preparation for the New Life Movement took place at our mission meeting in 1957. As a young missionary just beginning his second term, I was invited to preach one of the messages for that week. My heart was bubbling with the excitement and joy of our experiences in Asahigawa and the vision God had given to us while there and on furlough in 1956. Many of the churches in the United States had responded enthusiastically to the idea of seeing a major city and nationwide crusade take place in Japan. Nevertheless, as I prepared for my message I found it difficult to know just how to present that challenge to the more experienced missionaries who would be listening. Dedicated and seasoned missionaries like Edwin Dozier, Maxfield Garrott, and others who had so much more experience than I would be present. I could not appear to be telling these veteran missionaries what ought to be done and how to do it. I could never share my burden and vision in that way!

I wanted my message to be centered on Matthew 7:7–11, "Ask and ye shall receive," praying that it would then be obvious that we should launch out and seek to present Christ to all Japan *now!* God is "not willing that any should perish" and "today is the day of salvation." As Japan missionaries, we had no alternative. We had to ask for all Japan now! I planned to refer to the many promises of God in His Word that gave us reason to *know* that when we ask, we can expect results.

With those thoughts in mind, I went to mission meeting and attended all of the sessions, praying and seeking God's leading about how I could share my message. The morning came when I was to preach. I was still afraid that I would be misunderstood. I stayed in my room until the last minute. Seated on the *tatami* floor with my Bible open before me, I kept asking the Lord to let me know just how I was to present my burden and the message. My burden and vision were clear, but I still did not know just how to present it.

Finally the bell rang. It was time for the worship service. I could hear the children charging down the stairs on the way to the nursery and the missionaries moving toward the auditorium. I was almost frantic, for I still had no understanding of how I could share my message without appearing to tell our seasoned missionaries what to do. I looked out of my window across the pine trees and continued in an attitude of prayer, seeking God's guidance. On that morning and in that hour, He gave me an assurance and an awareness of His presence that was not only sufficient for that service but was deeply meaningful for me throughout the next seven years of the New Life Movement preparation. Among other things, He gave me a love for our mission and for every person present in that auditorium, as well as a new love for Japan, and a deepening of the conviction that we could reach Japan *now*. The Lord finally gave me my sermon topic, "Victory over Odds." This became the focus of all my preaching from that day until now! I could reassure myself and all present that if we would only ask and launch out in faith, He would provide the power, the resources, and the results! It was the message God had given me, not for that hour only but for any hour, anywhere and anytime. It was a message asking us to present the gospel to the entire city of Tokyo and to expect God to give the victory. I have never been more certain of His presence at any time in my entire ministry.

Following the message, a beloved and respected missionary, Bob Culpepper, stood with tears streaming down his cheeks and said, "I move that we ask our treasurer, George Hays, to begin withholding funds from our salary each month to be put in a fund called the Tokyo Citywide Revival Fund." It was a day and time for rejoicing! It was not the end of the battle but the beginning of one for which the Lord would ultimately give joyous victory! *We were slowly but surely approaching the idea of Partnership Evangelism.* We would begin finding the best possible ways of reaching the most people with the message of Christ *now*. Most important, we were recognizing that our God was able to do all things, if we could only believe and ask. That was a major step forward!

Facing Facts

For such an effort, a large sum of money would be needed, and there were already many urgent needs the missionaries and missions had officially presented to Southern Baptists that had not yet been met. It was understandable that when this unexpected additional request for funds and personnel was presented, neither the mission nor the Foreign Mission Board was prepared, thus the funds were not available. We needed 150 teams of at least three persons each to go into all 150 churches of our Japan Baptist Convention. We wanted a preacher, a musician, and a layman on each of these teams. In the five major area campaigns in Japan, Billy Graham was to climax those in Fukuoka, Osaka, Nagoya, Sapporo, and Tokyo.

We would need at least $350,000, and possibly more! No funds were available, and at that time there was no way in Southern Baptist life for a missionary to go directly to the national convention or a state convention and ask for personnel or funds. Here again circumstances indicated that there would be no money and no personnel for such a project. This is where Matthew 7:7–11 came into focus again! Even though there was no reasonable possibility for us to receive such a large amount of money, we would ask and believe!

During the Tokyo Baptist Church dedication in November 1959, we had shared our vision and burden for Tokyo and Japan with each participating Southern Baptist leader. Ramsey Pollard, president of the Southern Baptist Convention, listened as we drove him across the city and said, "Surely God would have us do something more toward reaching this city than what we're doing."

T. A. Patterson and the other convention leaders made clear that they, too, had the burden and the vision of what God *could* do if we would just call on Him. We all agreed to pray and ask.

A Historic Breakfast Meeting in St. Louis

One of the answers to our prayer came on furlough a year later in the form of a breakfast planned for the leaders of the Southern Baptist Convention. It became one of the most significant meetings in preparation for the New Life Movement. It was scheduled for the Third Baptist Church during the SBC annual meeting.

Doris and I had been extremely busy on furlough, going from church to church and from city to city, talking about the possibility of sharing Christ with the entire nation of Japan. Our five children were often loaded into our station wagon and accompanied us as we went from church to church. On some occasions my mother and father were brave enough to invite us to leave the children with them. On this particular occasion we had left our children with my parents, loaded our bags and the giant pictures of Tokyo into the back of a Buick station wagon, and started for St. Louis and the meeting to present the Tokyo challenge to the leaders of the Southern Baptist Convention.

Before leaving Japan for America and furlough, I had gone to the headquarters of the Mitsui Company in Japan. They had some beautiful, enlarged pictures of modern Japan mounted on boards, and I asked them to lend them to me to show to our folks at home. Amazingly, they agreed and we had brought with us on our flight home a beautiful aerial view of modern Tokyo, measuring eight feet by ten feet, together with several pictures of modern Japan measuring two feet by three feet. Those pictures said better than I could that we would have to make our best and most effective presentation if we were going to expect to reach Japan for

Christ. Pan American Airlines flew the pictures home for us at no charge, and we had them strapped on top of our station wagon as we traveled to St. Louis.

During the month before this convention, we had planned a breakfast meeting in order to share the challenge with every leader we had ever known. Most of those leaders had already made strong supportive comments concerning the urgency of making an effective presentation of the gospel in Japan. However, we felt that it was urgent for them to make those statements in public and before one another.

More than ninety convention leaders and friends had accepted our invitation. This included Southern Baptist Convention presidents, past and present; the Texas Baptist Convention leaders, past and present; all five of the seminary presidents; the Brotherhood Commission director; the Home Mission Board secretary; the Southern Baptist Convention executive secretary; and on and on until we had literally all of the major Southern Baptist Convention leaders pledged to come! This was an accomplishment that God alone could have brought about! Along with this leadership was a nucleus of concerned missionaries, friends, and Tokyo Baptist Church members who had been praying and longing for this evangelistic emphasis for many years. Tokyo Baptist Church members also served as ushers for the breakfast. Gerald and Inez Martin brought Baker James Cauthen, our Foreign Mission Board's executive secretary, and his wife Eloise. It was a gathering of God's leaders in the SBC of that day!

As we drove on toward St. Louis in preparation for this gathering of leaders, we had the burden of knowing we had invited all of these friends for breakfast at our expense! Actually, we barely had enough cash to buy gas to get there. We had a deep conviction that this meeting was of God, and we knew that if it was, He would provide. This was a principle that we had followed all of our lives. If we were going to expect God's power to perform miracles in giving us a nationwide campaign, we could not fear that He would fail to provide breakfast for one hundred people. We had sent out beautiful, gold-edged invitations, and all had accepted except the Cauthens. Dr. Cauthen's schedule was such that he was not certain that he would be able to be present. Nevertheless, we had printed our programs with the hope and a prayer that he would be able to be our closing speaker.

On our way to St. Louis, I stopped at a service station for gas and to make a call to my parents in Abilene to check on the children. Mother informed me that all was well and read a letter to me that had come from G. M. Cole, a pastor friend and college classmate who had been praying for our ministry through the years. Pastor Cole's letter had said that knowing of our need, he had asked William Fleming if he could help. Mr. Fleming had responded by sending a check to cover the cost of the breakfast in St. Louis! Again, without budget, sufficient personnel, and adequate understanding, God had given the victory.

The breakfast meeting was everything we had prayed for and more! K. Owen White, soon to be president of the Southern Baptist Convention, presided and stated boldly that there *must* be a major presentation of the gospel in Japan. Paul Stephens, director of the Radio and Television Commission, spoke strongly of the urgency of this effort. T. A. Patterson and C. Wade Freeman, with warmth and power, expressed the total commitment of Texas Baptists for the effort. All five seminary presidents, together with George Schroeder, executive secretary of the Brotherhood Commission, pledged total support. Dr. Schroeder said, "I know if we are ever to enlist our men for the Master, it will be through an all-out attempt to do the big and unusual thing for Christ."

New Life Movement speaksers: Ramsey Pollard (upper left);
T. A. Patterson (upper right); K. Owen White (lower left);
C. Wade Freeman (lower right)

It became evident that not one leader in the Southern Baptist Convention would want to see anything less than this major presentation made in Japan. Late in the program, Gerald and Inez Martin arrived with the Cauthens. Dr. Cauthen stood and, with the warmth and compassion that was always his, challenged the entire group with the idea of a great nationwide presentation of the gospel for Japan in 1963. The New Life Movement was truly under way!

More Encouraging Support

While on furlough in 1961, I was in a different church almost every day, and I do not remember being in one church that did not respond in a positive way to this idea of a nationwide campaign in Japan. A pastor in Greenville, South Carolina, said he felt that it was the greatest challenge in his generation. In Mississippi, the pastor of a small church just outside of Vicksburg said that never in his ministry had anything gripped his heart as had the challenge of the Japan New Life Movement. People were praying, and God was answering. Herschel Hobbs as president of the convention stated time and time again, "This is the golden hour of opportunity." At the close of every service on furlough in 1961, without exception, people came by, gripping my hand and pledging their prayers, saying, "We are praying for you and for the work there, and for this campaign."

Meeting Japan's Prime Minister

One of the most encouraging events in preparation for the New Life Movement campaign came during our furlough in 1961. President Kennedy had invited Prime Minister Hayato Ikeda to America, and I began to wonder just what he would see and experience while here. I envisioned his many cocktail parties and banquets with the leaders of government and industry and feared he might never see what makes our country great.

T. A. Patterson, executive director of our Baptist General Convention of Texas, was one with a great burden and concern for the coming campaign in Japan. I called and asked him if he would consider meeting with the prime minister and let him know just what was important to us and what made our country great. He immediately began calling our senators and the state department to set up the meeting. Many days went by, and it appeared that the meeting would not be confirmed in time to meet him before he returned to Japan.

One afternoon my phone rang in Abilene and the voice on the other end said, "This is Vice President Lyndon Johnson's office. He has asked me to call and see if you would be able to meet with Prime Minister Ikeda on his last stop in America, at Travis Air Force Base in California." I was shocked, for I had hoped that one of our Baptist leaders could have met with him. As a poor missionary without one dime in my pocket to buy a ticket to California, I said, "Yes, I will be glad to go!" I was thinking, *Even though I am not well known, and he will not know me from Adam, he will know that the vice president of the world's strongest nation thought enough of our religion and faith to ask him to meet with a missionary.* That was really the message I wanted the prime minister to get and take back with him anyway.

The problem was buying a ticket and getting there! I was scheduled to preach at First Baptist Church, Brownfield, Texas, on Sunday and to leave for California on Monday. After the first service on Sunday morning, Pastor Ed Crow and I met in his study for prayer and preparation for the second service. He said, "Dub, how do you travel all over and do these things on a missionary's salary?" I said, "God just takes care of it." He would not leave it alone and asked, "How does He take care of it?" He had finally asked a question that I was not ready to answer, so I said, "I am not sure." I will never forget Ed's reply when he said, "Well I know. We will take up an offering this morning!" It was one of the best offerings I had ever received! It was more than enough to pay for the round-trip air fare and the heavy phone bill that had been connected with trying to get someone to meet with the prime minister.

On the way to California, I prayed and asked the Lord to give me the right words to share with the Japanese leader. Carl Halvarson, my good friend and longtime missionary in Japan, met my plane and drove me to the air base. After meeting with the commanding officer, we drove to the ramp and waited for the prime minister and his family to land. In just a few moments, Air Force One landed, and the prime minister with his interpreter and aides began walking down the stairs toward us. I heard the interpreter whisper in the prime minister's ear, "This is the base commander," as he shook the general's hand. I had been stationed next to the general, and again I heard the interpreter say to the prime minister, "This is the missionary that Vice President Lyndon Johnson wanted you to meet!" From that moment on, I knew that our goal had already been reached. The prime minister knew that our leaders in government had great confidence in Christianity. It would have to be a real help to us back in Japan.

I showed the general my notes and asked if I would have any opportunity to share them with the prime minister. He said, "We do not have anything planned for him, so when we get to the officer's club, all the time is yours!"

At the officer's club, the general welcomed the prime minister again, then turned to me to share my words for him. The room was filled with American and Japanese press, and all of them seemed to have cameras with the old-fashioned flashbulbs going off constantly. I do not have the copy of my words, but the gist of the message was this: "Mr. Prime Minister, we are thrilled to have you in our country, and before you leave, we wanted to have just this moment to tell you what we in America think our most valuable asset is. It is not our oil, our industries, or our educational institutions. Our most valuable asset is our religious freedom and our faith in Christ!" I had wanted to talk to him in Japanese, but

I knew my Japanese would not be perfect, so I had spoken in English with the prime minister's interpreter whispering in his ear as I spoke.

When I had finished, the prime minister said, "Can I say a few words?" He said, "I, too, believe that the greatest need we have in Japan is a spiritual need, and we are glad you are there as a missionary. When you return, please come to see

Presenting Texas footware to Japanese Prime Minister Ikeda

me at the official residence." He went on to say, "Recently my wife and I were hiring a maid for our home, and we had two applications to consider—one was a Christian and one was not. We hired the Christian!"

I had brought some small gifts and proceeded to give them to him. As a Texan I had the honorary citizenship certificate, making the prime minister a Texan. And to go with it some cowboy boots and hat. He immediately sat down on the couch and put on the boots and hat. Because the prime minister had spoken to me in Japanese and the press had not heard his response to my speech, he turned to his interpreter again and said, "Tell the press what I said!" Then the interpreter told the combined press that the prime minister had said that he too thought that the greatest need for Japan was spiritual.

That night as I returned to Dallas, changed planes in Los Angeles, and looked down on the stack of newspapers, the first page of the *Wall Street Journal* showed me seated with the prime minister, putting on the boots and hat. The caption was, "East

Meets West," giving the story of the prime minister and the missionary.

After our return to Japan, I met the prime minister in his official residence in Tokyo, together with my coworker, Pastor Shuichi Matsumura. We gave him a Bible and had a time of prayer. Prime Minister Ikeda died shortly after our meeting. We were grateful for that privilege and the prime minister's promise to read the Bible.

Texas Baptist Vision for Campaign

T. A. Patterson of the Baptist General Convention of Texas, after prayerful consideration, courageously pledged to raise the money for the campaign. We thought we would need at least $300,000 and possibly $500,000. We even thought that the need might be a million dollars. Nevertheless, Dr. Patterson did not flinch! He was determined that whatever was needed would be provided. It could not have been done without his faith and leadership in America.

Walter Smyth, coordinating director of the Billy Graham crusades, said that he and Dr. Graham had been talking and praying and had decided to offer an additional three days for the campaign in Japan. This meant that Dr. Graham would be with us from March 31 through April 12. God was providing the greatest evangelistic leader in the history of our world because Christians had prayed and asked. Dr. Graham said that in all his recent campaigns in South America, he was almost constantly greeted by people saying, "We are praying for you and for the campaign in Japan."

While we were rejoicing over these daily miracles, yet another one was in the making. The American embassy called to tell me that Prime Minister Hayato Ikeda had worked out a time for me to meet with him at his residence at 1:30 P.M. that same day! The call came to me at noon, but by 1:30 P.M. we had a beautifully engraved Bible ready, and Pastor Matsumura and I proceeded to the official residence and presented the Bible, had prayer, and received words of assurances from him of his support of this campaign. As he promised to read the

Shuichi Matsumura and Billy Graham

Bible, he said, "I cannot emphasize one religion over another, but I am happy to know about the plans for the crusade next year. This is greatly needed in Japan."

Everyone believed, prayed, expected, and looked forward to the coming of the New Life Movement in 1963. No wonder more than 25,000 people in Japan came forward saying, "I'd like to know Christ as Lord and Savior." In 1957, at Tokyo Baptist Church, we had prayed saying, "Lord, let us see 15,000 to 25,000 people come to receive you in this campaign!" I wonder what would have happened had we had faith to pray and ask for 15 to 25 million people! He has said, "According to your faith, be it done unto you!"

The Miracle of the Movie

Ramsey Pollard, president of the Southern Baptist Convention, who would be presiding over the convention sessions in Miami, Florida, in June 1960, told me that if I could make a movie on modern Japan, with a challenge for this crusade, he would make sure that it was shown at the convention. The idea began when I had said to him, "If Southern Baptists could just *see* Japan as it really is instead of as they have remembered it, they would know what has to be done!" I had never made a movie and had no budget for one. I just had a dream and a prayer—but God began to provide!

One morning soon after Dr. Pollard left, I walked down to my mailbox and opened a letter from my cousins, Mr. and Mrs. Herb Reynolds. In the envelope was a check for three thousand dollars. This was very rare, for our support came to us through the Foreign Mission Board, and we did not call on our friends or family for funds. I ran back up the stairs to share the good news with Doris. God had just provided the money for the movie that would be shown at the Southern Baptist Convention. My heart was pounding!

I went immediately to the Nippon Eiga Shinsha Movie Company, the equivalent to our American Movietone News. This was the largest and most famous movie news company in Japan, a branch of the Asahi News Corp, the largest news gathering agency in the world. I met with the president, Mr. Horiba, concerning my desire to make a movie on modern Japan. Mr. Horiba listened for a while and said, "Nobody wants to see a movie on modern Japan." I explained to him that all the movies made by the airlines and travel agencies showed Japan as a backward country with cherry blossoms, Mount Fuji, wooden clogs, umbrellas, paper walls, and rice paddies but did not show the progress that had taken place. I said, "Mr. Horiba, Japan is beautiful, and that's the way people of America see your country, but that's not all Japan is today!" (Remember, this was 1959.) I told him, "We need a color movie of at least twenty minutes' duration on modern Japan. I do not want an umbrella, bicycle, or a wooden shoe in the film. I don't even want Mount Fuji or the cherry blossoms. I want to show the aggressive, great, and booming economy of Japan. That is really Japan today." I continued, saying, "I want to show the Nikon and Canon camera companies in Japan, the Toyota automobile agency, the shipbuilding industry, and the bullet trains—everything that is modern and that is growing. We must let the Americans know what Japan is really like!" Finally he said, "I believe we could do that. Would you want it in color?" I said, "It has to be in color, and of the best possible quality." Finally he said, "We'll make it."

After another discussion on the price, he said it would cost us $12,500! I was not prepared for that. I had been naive, of course. I knew that a roll of film cost only $5.95. How in the world could they use up $12,500 worth of film on such a short movie! In a call to the States, I told Paul Stephens of our Radio and Television Commission what they had said. He said, "That is just half of what it would have cost in the States! It is a reasonable price." However, at that moment I said to Mr. Horiba, "I'm very sorry that I've taken your time. I only have three thousand dollars—two thousand for the movie and one thousand to buy prints to be shown in the churches across America." I told him, "I still think that you need that kind of movie on Japan."

It was amazing, but in less than a week I had a call from Mr. Horiba, and he said, "Come back. We want to talk with you about the movie." I started not to go because I knew I didn't have any more money then than I had the first time we had talked, and there seemed to be little reason for going. I thought they had come up with some plan to get my three thousand dollars, even though we could not make the movie. Nevertheless, without much faith, I went back to meet with them. I even left the motor running as I double-parked my car on a busy downtown Tokyo street and ran up the stairs to Mr. Horiba's office. When I went into the room, there sat Mr. Horiba, the president, and two of the directors around a low coffee table, with the inevitable hot tea already poured. Two contracts had been typed out in English and were lying on the table. They said, "We, too, believe we need that movie, and Japan needs it. We will make it. We will pay $10,000 and you pay $2,000." I could not believe it. Again, God had provided. When circumstances had said no, God had said yes. We began to make the movie.

Mr. Horiba gave me the privilege of writing the script and directing the film from beginning to end. What a joy to select the best of Japan in color and share it with the people of America. Later that same year Governor Ryotaro Azuma of Tokyo took this film with him to Rome and, with a different sound track, presented Tokyo's bid for the 1964 Olympics. I had not had one picture of a church in the film, for even one church in a twenty-minute film would have distorted the view of the Christian presence in Japan. This was a country with only one-half of one percent of the population Christian! The film showed only the economic progress of Japan. Of course our sound track gave the Christian challenge.

I had proposed that the film begin at Haneda Airport with a Boeing 707 jet screaming across the screen and close after showing the miraculous story of Japan's great economic revival. The last scene was to be of the empty Olympic stadium, where I would make an appeal to Southern Baptists to send the people needed to help us fill the stadium and present the gospel of Jesus Christ in the world's largest city while we still had the opportunity. God blessed, and in addition to those scenes, Governor

Azuma himself appeared in the film and welcomed the Christians of the world to come and help in the battle for eternal hope for the salvation of the Japanese people.

Evidence of God's leading while making the movie came in many ways. I had asked the camera crew to go to the Haneda International Airport and put their camera on the ground beside the active runway to catch a Pan American 707 jet flash by in landing. One evening just at dinner time, they called me and said the airport officials would not let them put the camera near the runway. I was still a reserve pilot in the Air Force and was familiar with flying in and out of Haneda, so I suggested that they get in a boat and place their cameras on the approach lights at the end of the runway. They could then film the 707 as it came directly toward them, filling the screen completely as it flashed overhead. That footage became the opening scene of a fast-moving movie on modern Japan.

On another occasion, I had asked the crew to film the lowering of the American flag at the American embassy just at sunset. Again they called and said, "We are here, and it is sunset, but the flag has already been taken down." I wanted to emphasize the fact that although we say we cannot send missionaries in great numbers to Japan, the business world had already sent ten thousand businessmen to Tokyo, and every major company in America was represented. This was in 1961. I wanted to point out that it was just the Christians who were slow in making a major presentation! I suggested that the camera crew ask the Marine guard if he would put the flag back up again. They asked him, and the guard cooperated. That picture appears in the movie, followed by clips of the neon lights showing the signs of Ford, Coca-Cola, and many other major American companies working in Japan. The message is clear: "Where are the aggressive American Christians if we believe that the message of Christ is the most important message to *be shared in the world today?*" Everyone cooperated in making that movie! Even Governor Azuma appeared and let me write his speech inviting Christians of the world to come and share the gospel in Tokyo! What a joy and thrill to watch the Lord work!

It was a God-given joy and miracle to see the film completed in time for the Southern Baptist Convention meeting in Miami, Florida. Dr. Pollard showed it before sixteen thousand amazed and surprised people at the convention. It had its divine effect! Baptists *did* understand the Tokyo challenge!

Oops! An Official Reprimand

I had no earthly idea that making a movie to be shown to Southern Baptists was in conflict with the principles of the Foreign Mission Board. The board reminded me that it was not the field missionary's responsibility to provide stateside promotion. I was not aware of any such rule but did know they wanted us to keep the people at home informed of what we were doing. In my hurt over the misunderstanding, I said to some of my friends, "It's not illegal to mimeograph our reports. It seems it is only illegal if you try to do it first class." Of course I understand better now the concerns of the Foreign Mission Board. They could not leave the stateside promotion up to each missionary. However, I am eternally grateful to Ramsey Pollard for requesting the movie and for his boldness in showing it to Southern Baptists at the convention. They were able to see firsthand the modern, booming Japan and its obvious need for the gospel.

I was more than encouraged when I received a letter, dated June 10, 1960, from Billy Graham saying, "We were all thrilled with the film you produced, which was shown at the [Southern

Baptist] Convention. I was given a copy and have shown it several times to my personal friends. Certainly the Lord gave you great wisdom in planning this film. It made a tremendous impact on me! I seriously doubt that I could have gotten a vision of the strategic importance of Tokyo had it not been for that film."

Winston Crawley, in a letter dated December 16, 1964, said that Daniel and Beverly O'Reagan, after seeing *The Tokyo Challenge,* had volunteered for missionary service in Japan. God was continuing to bless every effort in preparation for the campaign.

Without any doubt, God had provided, and we were able to see again that He would provide when we called in faith.

No Budget, No Personnel, No Understanding

I have rarely been a part of any significant or meaningful program that had an adequate budget, adequate personnel, or complete understanding for the project. Just as was true in making the movie, in carrying out the citywide crusade in Asahigawa, and in building Tokyo Baptist Church, I made my commitment before the resources or way to victory could be seen.

Likewise, in the New Life Movement there was no budget, no personnel, and little understanding of the program, but God gave 549 dedicated laymen, musicians, and preachers from America to execute the program, and almost $800,000 to support the campaign. Twenty years after its inception, Partnership Evangelism was adopted by the Southern Baptist Foreign Mission Board. I think it is important to note that in each of these endeavors, God gave the victory even though we had *none* of the so-called ingredients necessary to experience a real victory!

Stretching Our Faith

Preparation for the New Life Movement generated genuine hope and joyous expectations. We began to think about asking for the Japan Philharmonic Orchestra to perform at the key meetings. Further along in preparation, our faith included the help of a university band and choirs from America. God gave it all!

We invited Billy Graham to come, and he agreed! Invitations went out to other Christian leaders, not only from America but from around the world. We invited Christian leaders from many fields of endeavor to present their testimony of what Christ meant to them. Thomas Frier, a Christian publisher from Georgia, was invited and came. Kenji Majima, one of the great Christian choir directors of our day, put together a Japanese choir that could match anything we could bring from America.

We invited well-known professional athletes from America to help us reach a nation getting ready for the 1964 Olympics. Carl Erskine of the Brooklyn Dodgers and Bobby Richardson of the New York Yankees came and made a monumental contribution. Wilma Rudolph, who won four gold medals in track and field, came to witness. Shelby Wilson, gold medal wrestler in the 1960 Rome Olympics, was especially well used in the campaign.

I was convinced that our preachers, missionaries, and laymen were more than able to bring the message that was needed, but we needed to attract people to the meetings. Billy Graham was the most effective and best-known minister in the world, and we wanted his message and help. We had determined to use television, radio, and the newspaper, whatever it cost. These well-known leaders and artists were a great help in appealing to the media.

In training and preparation for the campaign, five hundred seminary students, pastors, and missionaries worked as counselors and helped in the follow-up.

The story of the preparation and the execution of the New Life Movement is a story of daily miracles and of God's presence and power. T. A. Patterson, prior to the New Life Movement, had become executive secretary of the Baptist General Convention of Texas and had shouldered the burden of making sure that the finances were provided. I remember when he told the Foreign Mission Board, "Texas Baptists will accept the responsibility of providing both funds and personnel if the Foreign Mission Board will approve it." Dr. Cauthen had said, "As long as you will promise not to take it out of the Lottie Moon Christmas Offering or out of the Cooperative Program, we will back it 100 percent!" Thus the barrier of no budget, no personnel, and little understanding was broken again. God used men of faith and courage like Patterson, who would be willing to launch out, to bring victory.

A First in Advertising and Publicity

To present the gospel in Japan, we met with Nobuo Ban, an executive with Dentsu, the world's largest advertising company. Together with Pastor Matsumura, we signed a $200,000 contract for nationwide publicity. This may have been a first in foreign missions! "Whatever it takes" had to be the commitment of all connected with the preparation. The Texas *Baptist Standard* made the first contribution of $12,500 toward the Dentsu fee of $200,000. Paul M. Stephens, director of the Southern Baptist Radio and Television Commission, in his detailed report to the convention, told the story of the church in Asahigawa in presenting the challenge of the New Life Movement to Southern Baptists.

Every convention leader, without reservation, gave total commitment to preparing for the Japan New Life Movement!

Should we want to see revival in any country where we work in the days ahead, this kind of commitment, "*Whatever* it takes," by *all* of His people, will *always* be necessary.

Japanese Leaders Come to the U.S. in 1963

In preparation for the Japan campaign, Southern Baptists invited seven Japanese leaders to visit America and help lay the burden of that campaign on the hearts of our people. On January 16, 1963, Toshio Miyoshi, president of the Japan Baptist Convention; Kiyoki Yuya, dean of Japanese pastors; Nobuo Arase, evangelism secretary; Shuichi Matsumura, chairman of the New Life Movement campaign; and Naka Hirano, professor of chemistry at International Christian University, all responded to the invitation of Southern Baptists and came to share their vision for the campaign.

Japanese Visit Abilene, Texas

A notable incident worthy of remembrance took place on the arrival of this group one cold January day at the Abilene Municipal Airport. Elwin Skiles, pastor of First Baptist Church in Abilene, and one of the spiritual leaders of that city, helped plan the reception. I explained to Dr. Skiles that if we were to impress the Japanese, we needed to welcome them in their way. They would recognize the meaning of our actions if, first of all, we *as a group,* would meet them at the airport when they arrived. Abilene responded! Over two hundred dedicated Abilene Christians braved the blustering north wind and went to the little airport in the midst of that January weather! As the plane carrying the Japanese pastors touched down, the mayor came to me and said,

"We have a problem. We have a famous movie star on board. He is coming to help with a fund-raising program for the West Texas Rehabilitation Center. How can we handle this?"

I had invited the Hardin-Simmons University Cowboy Band, the mayor of Abilene, and several other city officials to be there to greet the Japanese delegation, so I suggested to the mayor that we ask the Japanese pastors to remain on board until the movie star had been welcomed. After his welcome, we would then let the Japanese come forward and be welcomed by the delegation that had gathered, primarily to meet *them*. I suppose not one of the two hundred people present even knew that the movie star was coming. To this day, I assume that the movie star, Cliff Robertson, is still talking about the great reception he received in a West Texas town when over two hundred people gathered in icy cold weather, with the Hardin-Simmons University Cowboy Band, to meet him. After Cliff Robertson was greeted, the officials asked the Japanese delegation to exit the plane and be met by the mayor and church officials. Spontaneously, all of these Abilene Christians lined up and went by, one at a time, to give the Japanese a handshake and a real warm west Texas greeting.

I noticed as I greeted Pastor Arase, who may have been a little anti-American and antimissionary in his thinking, that there was a little tear in his eye. I assumed it was the result of the blowing cold wind. We boarded the official cars with the flashing red and green lights to go into the city to see what we had been touting as one of the greatest Christian cities in the world! No beer or whiskey was served in our city at that time, and there were no taverns or bars permitted! We wanted to show them the three Christian colleges, the Baptist hospital, and perhaps more churches per capita than in any other place in the world. In those days all stores were closed on Sunday. It was certainly one of the finest Christian towns in the world. My, what a change today!

The Japanese were more than just impressed. Dr. Skiles had arranged for the Hilton Hotel to provide rooms, and they had just remodeled their suites in a Japanese motif. Each room had special entries, called *genkans* in Japan! It was a perfect reception for our group. After they had rested a few minutes in their rooms, I went around to tell them we were ready to tour America's Christian city! When I came to the door where missionary Coleman Clarke and Pastor Arase were staying, Pastor Arase was lying on the bed with a towel across his face, still weeping. He said, in referring to the two hundred Abilene Christians he had just met at the airport, "I didn't know they cared so much." That reception changed Pastor Arase's attitude toward Americans and missionaries forever.

Years after the Abilene experience, whenever I would sit down with Pastor Arase, he would put his head in his hands and pause for a moment to regain composure, remembering the compassion and love expressed to them by those West Texans. I believe that experience was more meaningful to the Japanese men than their meeting with President Kennedy a few days later in the White House. Everyone went all out to be sure the Japanese visitors knew we were ready to come and share the gospel. How we long today to see such a concern and interest expressed again. It is possible, and it is desperately needed *now!*

God Provides Tokyo's Famous Stadium

Among the daily victories that God provided in the preparation and execution of the New Life Movement was the obtaining of a stadium for the closing meeting in Tokyo. Knowing that Billy Graham was one of those scheduled to preach, we wanted to have the Korakuen Stadium, Japan's number-one sports center. It was the Madison Square Garden and Yankee Stadium of Japan. We spoke with the stadium manager and were told that it was not available. We went from one stadium to another until we had examined every major stadium in Tokyo, and all had said no. We were running out of time and still had no meeting place. The massive publicity needed the name and location of the stadium before Dentsu could complete their printing. Billy Graham was coming, the campaign was scheduled, but no stadium! Finally, Pete Gillespie and I decided to go back and talk with one of the stadium managers in Shibuya one more time. Again he said, "Our stadium is not available, but why don't you speak to the manager of the Korakuen Stadium?" I said, "We have already asked him, and he has said it is not possible." He said, "I have talked with him recently, and I think you should go back and ask him again."

With this bit of encouragement, Pete and I went back to the Korakuen Center to meet the young manager again. When we arrived he was out, but his secretary graciously invited us in and ordered us a delicious Chinese dinner while we waited. The hospitality was unbelievable. When the manager came in, we shared again our need for the stadium. He said, "First of all, we are installing new lights and making some renovations in preparation for the fast-approaching baseball season, and we cannot have these new lights ready in time for your meeting." An inspiration hit me and I said, "We are not going to chase fly balls. We are just going to read hymns and the Bible, and we don't need that kind of lighting."

Somewhere in our discussion, and I'm not sure where, God spoke to his heart. He said, "I don't think you need our stadium. I don't believe people will come in these numbers." "Yes," I said, "they will come, and this is what God would have us do." Finally he said, "OK, and I'll tell you what I am going to do. We'll let you have the stadium, but I'm concerned about your attendance, so I will give an order to our seven hundred employees telling them that they have to attend!" The Lord took control of this discussion, and the manager said, "I think you will also need some bunting and the flags to make your campaign a truly festive occasion, so I will provide that at no cost!" From no stadium, and no possibility of a stadium, to approval for Japan's best in just over one hour! Not only a stadium, but one with seven hundred persons already guaranteed in attendance and all the trimmings for a special occasion! It was absolutely thrilling to stand on the sidelines and watch the Lord perform miracle after miracle in answer to the prayers of God's people for revival. We have not because we ask not!

The Olympic Star Comes

On one occasion I telexed back to Texas asking T. A. Patterson to locate an Olympic star who could come and appeal to the Japanese, who were feverishly preparing for the 1964 Olympics. Dr. Patterson replied saying that Shelby Wilson, an Olympic gold medal winner in the 1960 Rome Olympics and a dedicated Christian, would be coming to witness during the campaign. I will have to admit that at first I was a little surprised and somewhat disappointed to learn that our Olympic star was a wrestler and not a runner. I was not at all sure about how we could use him. I carried the name Shelby Wilson in my shirt pocket for several days before I could decide what to do with him.

Finally I asked my secretary, Miss Eileen Sanno, a *Nisei* from Lanai, Hawaii, to look up the phone number of Japan's Wrestling Association. Even those who are familiar with a Japanese telephone directory can sometimes have difficulty in finding a number. I had absolutely no confidence in the number she would give

*Mr. Shibata, chairman of World Wrestling Association (standing)
with Shelby Wilson to his left*

to me, but she soon gave me what was supposed to be the number for the chairman of Japan's Wrestling Association. I added it to Shelby Wilson's name and placed it back in my pocket.

The busy preparation schedule increased, but finally I decided I must make that call. I dialed the number Miss Sanno had given me, and a man answered. I explained to him in Japanese that I was W. H. Jackson and was with the Japan Baptist Convention, calling about an Olympic gold medal wrestler that we would soon bring to Japan. I told him that, as chairman of the Japan and World Wrestling Association, he was welcome to use the champion in any way he might choose, so long as he would give him an opportunity to tell why he came to Japan. He replied in almost perfect English, saying, "Could you tell me the name of your wrestler?" I said, "His name is Shelby Wilson. He defeated a Japanese in the finals in Rome when he won the gold medal." Then Mr. Shibata, the chairman said, "Oh, yes. I know him very well. He and my son were roommates at Oklahoma A&M!"

Can you imagine the odds against such a victory from one phone call, in a city of ten million people after searching through a Japanese phone book in the world's largest city? God gave us, in a most spectacular way, the exact man at the right moment. Shelby was so effective during the campaign that the Japanese asked him to stay over, and God used him on national television as he stayed to help train the Japanese teams in preparation for the Olympics. Because of these miracles and many more, we cannot but believe that "all things are possible" when God is leading! I can never accept the comment that "It is impossible to go," regardless of the circumstances, when such a comment is made after God has already said, "Go." If He has spoken and it is His will, it is impossible to fail if we look to Him in faith and trust.

Another Miracle in Preparation

Japan was fast becoming one of the television capitals of the world. There were six major television networks and channels broadcasting in Tokyo every day in 1962. None of them carried the Christian message, and the cost of TV time in Japan was even greater than time on our major networks in America. We prayed daily and asked for God's guidance and access to TV in Japan.

During the Christmas season in 1962, four months before the New Life Movement, I was driving through Tokyo listening to the Armed Forces Radio Network. I tuned in just in time to hear a newsman say that Charlton Heston was visiting Japan in connection with the showing of his film. I thought how wonderful it would be if we could get him to read the Christmas story on national TV! Dentsu, in signing our contract, had said that if we should have a program worthy of national TV from their viewpoint, they would give us air time for a Christmas program. Charlton Heston was the best-known movie star in all Japan at that time. Even as I drove through the traffic that day, Tokyo's finest theaters were crowded with standing-room-only audiences in order to see him as Moses in *The Ten Commandments*. He was the number-one box-office attraction in Japan. Everyone knew Charlton Heston.

As soon as I arrived home, I called my dear friend, Paul Stephens, back in the United States and asked for his advice. He thought the best approach would be for me to call Mr. Heston directly in his room in the Okura Hotel. I placed the call and explained to his personal

Charlton Heston reads the Christmas story on Japanese national television, as Shuichi Matsumura interprets

secretary that we had been given national television time for a Christmas program, and would Mr. Heston be willing to read the Christmas story on national television for us? The secretary said, "I believe that Mr. Heston would be more than glad to do this if his schedule permits. He has a very heavy schedule, and he has many commitments for tomorrow," which was the only day he had left. "He has an interview scheduled on a television cooking school program tomorrow morning, and if that program happens to be on the same channel you plan to use for the Christmas story, I think that he'll be glad to do it." I held my breath and asked him, praying, "What channel is he scheduled to be on for the interview?" He said, "Channel 4." That was the channel that had offered us the nationwide Christmas program and was the most popular and the strongest commercial channel in Tokyo. Praise the Lord! In two phone calls the most famous American personality in all of

Japan had agreed to read the Christmas story on national television for us, and it would not cost one penny!

I borrowed a pulpit stand from Tokyo Baptist Church, called a painter, and had him paint the New Life Movement logo on a board that we could place on the speaker's stand Mr. Heston would use. It read, "Merry Christmas from the Japan Baptist Convention New Life Movement." Early the next morning I picked up the pulpit stand with the freshly painted emblem, put it in the trunk of my car, and rushed it to the studio just in time to see Mr. Charlton Heston finish his interview on the cooking program. The cameraman turned forty-five degrees to focus on the pulpit and the New Life Movement sign. I introduced Mr. Heston to Pastor Shuichi Matsumura, our chairman, and greeted Mrs. Heston and their son, thanking them for his willingness to share this Christmas story on television. I handed him a double-spaced typewritten copy of the Christmas story that I had prepared to make it easier for him to read. He studied it, making a few marks for emphasis, and then began to read!

He had grown a long beard in preparation to play John the Baptist for his forthcoming movie *The Greatest Story Ever Told* so we felt that all was certainly in order! I have never heard the story read more effectively by any pastor or Christian leader in all my life! The studio went silent as he read. When he finished, there were tears in the eyes of some of the cameramen, recognizing the presence and the power of the Lord. The Christmas story had just been shared on national television all over Buddhist Japan! What a thrill! I told Charlton Heston that if his movie business ever fell through, I thought we could work him into our missionary program. His wife replied, "I don't know of anything I'd rather see Charlton do than be involved in the Christian effort."

Again, in spite of an impossible situation, no budget, and no program, God had given us a national television program free of charge. It was so well received that the Charlton Heston Christmas reading was repeated three

With New Life Movement speakers Herschel Hobbs (left) and Baker James Cauthen (center)

times, and in some cities six times, all over Japan. *God is able* when all seems hopeless. I pray we will never forget that.

At times we faced what appeared to be insurmountable obstacles. In the closing stages of our preparation for the New Life Movement, just six weeks before the campaign was to begin, and after seven years of intensive preparation, Billy Graham became ill and had to cancel! Our Japanese preparation committee called an emergency session—and some were calling for a cancellation. As much as we had wanted Dr. Graham—in fact, no one could take his place—I felt led to say, "This is our opportunity to see how God can give victory without His number-one servant, Dr. Graham!" We called on Baker James Cauthen, executive secretary of our own Foreign Mission Board, to take Dr. Graham's place, and God gave the victory anyway! We missed Dr. Graham, but a whole nation learned that "all things are possible to him that believeth," with or without the world's greatest preacher! Dr. Graham would have been the first to say that revival comes from the Lord, not the preacher. We learned a very valuable lesson.

A Japanese Church Accepts the Challenge

Ichikawa was a Tokyo suburb of 200,000 people and home of a new mission pastored by Nobuo Togami. He had invited me to come and present the challenge of the New Life Movement. The church had seven members, but eleven persons were present for the morning service. I had planned to urge them to have a citywide crusade! When I looked at this little group gathered in the pastor's front room and looked at my sermon subject, "With God All Things Are Possible," I almost changed my sermon! Surely this small group could not reasonably be expected to launch a citywide crusade. All eleven were young people, all except the elderly lady playing the organ. All of us sat on the tatami mats, praying as the music began.

I leaned back against the wall and looked out across the rice paddies that surrounded the little parsonage in the suburbs of Ichikawa. I prayed, "Oh, Lord, how can we have a citywide crusade with no more than this to work with?" Nevertheless, the Lord led me to go on and preach the message, "All things are possible if we only believe!" The message began, "'Ask and ye shall receive.' Do you want a citywide crusade in Ichikawa?" It was thrilling to see and sense the confidence of the pastor and his little band of believers during that service. It was evident that God was present; He had spoken, the people had heard, and decisions had been made. One decision had been to have a citywide crusade!

A few days later I received a phone call from Pastor Togami. In an excited voice he said, "You'll be thrilled to know that we have secured the city auditorium, a steel-and-concrete building that seats eighteen hundred people!" I thought, *What a tremendous thing for seven members of a new mission in a Buddhist city to do! They rented the city auditorium!*

A few days later I had another call and the pastor said, "We have gone to the finest musical organization in our city, and their choir has agreed to come and sing for our crusade. None of them are Christian, but we believe we'll win some of them to Christ." I said, "Praise the Lord" and rejoiced with him again. In another few days he called again and said, "We have located the finest orchestra in Ichikawa, and they are going to come and play for our meeting! We now have the city auditorium, the orchestra, and the choir preparing for this major outreach!" My heart pounded with joy to know that God's people in Ichikawa and across Japan were, in faith, preparing for a major harvest that the Lord would give.

There is more. Near the Harajuku area in Tokyo, where many foreigners go to shop, there is a store called the Oriental Bazaar. One morning, as Doris and I were shopping, I looked up and caught a glimpse of a couple at the back of the store. With my longtime interest in the Brooklyn Dodgers and the New York Yankees, I thought I recognized Don Newcomb, the great Brooklyn Dodgers pitcher. I knew that he had just been signed by the Nagoya Dragons to come to Japan and pitch for the Japanese team. I went over and said, "Aren't you Don Newcomb of the Brooklyn Dodgers?" He said, "Yes." I replied, "Mr. Newcomb, while you are in Japan, I hope you will find some churches here and share your testimony. You are better known after only thirteen days in Japan than I am after thirteen years." He said, "I'll be glad to! How do I go about it?" I said, "I'll find a church that will invite you to come out and share your Christian testimony." He said, "When?" and I said, "Whenever you are ready." He shocked me when he said, "What about next Sunday?"

I had just spoken in the Ichikawa Baptist Church the week before, when Pastor Togami and his seven members had expressed tremendous faith in getting ready for the New Life Movement. I thought, *Why not give them one of America's greatest baseball heroes this next Sunday!* It is a testimony of what God thinks of the faith of a church when He gives them one of baseball's most famous players to testify the next Sunday after they vote to do the impossible! Only the Lord can move that fast and in that way to give that kind of victory!

The next Sunday morning, Doris and I took Don Newcomb to the service, but the church had not had time to announce his coming. Pastor Togami dismissed the congregation and told them to go out and get their autograph books and invite their neighbors to come back in thirty minutes. They filled the building! When my time came to introduce Don Newcomb, I shared with them what he meant to American baseball—and of course everyone knows how the Japanese love baseball! When Don stood up, his testimony was very short, very straight, very simple, and shocking. All he said was, "What the reverend says is right. Do it!" And he sat down. How wonderful it was to be in the midst of a program that God has directed and to watch Him provide when we were absolutely incapable of doing what needed to be done. God is able. "All things are possible to him that believeth." What are we asking for?

That small band of new Christians boldly prepared, and God gave them a good team from Texas including Bailey Stone as their preacher and Harold Davis as their musician. God also blessed by letting them see over 350 persons come forward in the campaign

Page 119, First service of the New Life Movement,
Waseda University auditorium, Tokyo
Page 120, Closing rally of the New Life Movement,
Korakuen, Tokyo

saying, "We would like to know Christ as Savior." From seven members to almost 350 professions of faith in one week! In Japan! In Buddhist Japan!

The Opening Rally

After seven years of prayer and preparation, the New Life Movement began. The 549 team members from America had arrived and found their places of service in Japan, Korea, Taiwan, the Philippines, Hong Kong, and Singapore. The New Life Movement for Japan opened in the Waseda University auditorium, where over three hundred of those American volunteers joined with the hundreds of dedicated Japanese Christians in singing and giving thanks to God for the revival we knew He was going to give! The Japan Philharmonic Orchestra was seated on one side of the huge platform, with the Hardin-Simmons University Band on the other, and a five-hundred-voice Japanese choir in the middle! We sat in awe, listened, and watched what the Lord had done and was doing! We felt that we had already gone on to glory!

I was seated next to Dr. Cauthen on the platform when he leaned over to me and said, "Dub, I believe this approach can be used in any major city of the world." I was thrilled to think that Southern Baptists would soon be on their way to using everyone in sharing an aggressive and positive message of love and salvation across the world. The wonderful results of the New Life Movement should have been encouragement enough to say to Southern Baptists, "This is something we can and must do over and over again all over the world!"

The prestigious Waseda University auditorium was filled to overflowing when the Cowboy Band marched down both aisles and took its place on the platform. Kurt Kaiser, vice president of

Word Records and one of America's leading music directors, led the choirs, the orchestra, the band, and the congregation in singing "How Great Thou Art" and "Amazing Grace." Guest speakers from Africa, India, and America took their places together with the laymen and laywomen in sharing their message and testimonies as the New Life Movement began and hundreds began to receive Christ as Lord and Savior.

Looking out across the vast crowd that had gathered for this unique service, I could see the glassed-in booths of the press section, where the Lord had provided for the Far East Broadcasting Company to come in and record, doing simultaneous translation into other Asian languages so that the messages could be shared by radio across Asia. More miracles and victories took place that evening than can be reported. God was present. His plans were being carried out. It was the opening salvo in a major evangelistic effort that would see more than 25,000 persons in Japan invite Christ into their lives!

A FARMER AND A POSTMAN

WOODROW AND VIVIAN LAWLIS were church members in Golan, Texas, near Abilene, where I led my first pastorate back in 1946. Their testimony encouraged many people across the world to become involved in Partnership Evangelism.

From the beginning of my ministry, I have been most impressed and inspired by the genuineness, love, and compassion of a humble Christian witness, whether from a preacher or a layman. Regardless of how true the message or how talented the speaker, if that spirit of love and humility is not clearly evident, I am troubled. The need of today's world is not a more skillful or a more talented presentation of the gospel but rather a more powerful, loving, and compassionate demonstration of God's presence in the life of those who share it.

When the New Life Movement became a real possibility, Florence Oldham Weaver of the Oldham Little Church Foundation in Houston offered to help six persons go, and she agreed to sponsor Woodrow. In those days people usually thought only of sending a denominational leader overseas. Certainly we wanted and needed those talented leaders, but I also wanted to involve other faithful and effective church members—just "ordinary Christians." I immediately called Woodrow and told him

Chapter 9

that we were going to have a major evangelistic campaign in Japan and that the key to it was involving laypeople. I asked him if he would be willing to go. I expected him to be a little hesitant, but he immediately said, "Yes. If the funds are available, I believe I should go." Several years later, he told me that after he hung up, he began to think about what he had said. *What on earth have I done? Why have I said that I would be willing to go to Japan? I don't feel adequate in presenting the gospel here at home. What in the world could I do in Japan?* Those are the kind of thoughts that run through the hearts and minds of almost all who considers participating in a campaign.

Woodrow questioned the stewardship of using $1,750 to take a farmer to Japan when it could have paid for some great preacher or musician. He had many questions about the value of his going, but there was never a question in *my* mind as to his value. People like Woodrow are the heart of Partnership Evangelism. It cannot be done without them! I have always felt that the greatest need and the most valuable tool to be employed in winning our world to Christ is the warmhearted, loving testimony of God's humble servants.

Even after Woodrow committed to go, he doubted that he should go. As the time to board the plane came nearer, his doubts and fears increased. *Almost every person participating in Partnership Evangelism has had to face these doubts and fears. Everyone needs to be ready for this battle.* After God makes clear to a person that he should go, Satan comes in to say, "This is a great plan, but it's not for you." Or, "This is something that ought to be done, but you are not the one to do it." Or, "Who do you think you are that you should go so far and spend so much money to share the gospel when the needs are so great right around you here? Look at your own life and your own needs. Why do you think you could help someone else? Don't you realize that there are many things that need to be done in your own life before you go to another country?" Over and over Satan has used all of these tools of doubt to discourage those determined to be a partner in sharing the gospel with the world.

Thank God that the Lord we serve and the Spirit of Christ that moves in His people is stronger than the darts and doubts that Satan uses to destroy the courage and testimony of those willing to go. Many churches overseas have requested a team and did not get one because an American church misunderstood God's leading and did not go. We thank God that we have seen more than ten thousand go, and now more than 33,000 are going each year!

Just a few days before the plane was to leave Dallas for Tokyo, Woodrow, in his sincere concern about his ability to be effective, went so far as to pray and explain to the Lord, "I'm not the one to go. Could you just break my leg? Then it would be perfectly legitimate for me to stay behind!" He was sincere, but the Lord did not answer that prayer. The night before the plane was to depart, Woodrow lay in his bed in a cold sweat, rolling and tossing, realizing that in a few hours he would be on a plane with hundreds of people going halfway around the world to share the gospel. The prayer he prayed that night was, "I am only a farmer without any special expertise, and it is obvious that I should not go. Lord, could you just give me a heart attack tonight so that I won't have to go? I do not want to waste that lady's money." What sincerity! But how wrong he was! God *did* want him in Japan, and he went.

Doris and I met the Boeing jets as they landed in Tokyo. We watched those hundreds of Americans get off those planes, including the Hardin-Simmons University Band. What a day!

How many times had we gone to the airport to meet one or two Christians or new missionaries who had come to help and had to hunt for them among the hundreds of business people who poured into Japan daily in the interest of their companies? Now, at least for one time, it was a thrill to be in an airport where practically everyone we saw was a God-called Christian who had come halfway around the world to witness for Christ. Likewise, those same Christians soon poured into the lobby of the Okura Hotel and fellowshipped with one another in anticipation of going out to witness! I was thrilled to look into the dining room of that five-star hotel and see men and women at almost every table thanking God for their health, their food, and for the privilege of being his ambassadors in Japan. Those sights will remain with us forever! I can still see these great buses pulling up in front of the hotel to carry loads of people to the Tokyo main station, where they would distribute tracts and invitations to the mass rally at the Tokyo Korakuen Sports Stadium. What a switch from our usual days as missionaries! What if they had not come!

I spotted Woodrow Lawlis as soon as he came into the airport terminal. I called out to him over the noise and confusion and said, "Woodrow, we can't visit now, but we look forward to having you in our home before you leave." He smiled, and I could tell he was nervous. I was overjoyed to see him there. A longtime dream had come true!

I assigned Woodrow to the Shinagawa Baptist Church between Tokyo and Yokohama. Pastor Nabekura had told me earlier, when he heard that I had assigned this farmer to his church, that I should consider reassigning him to another church. His church, although small, was centered in probably the most industrialized section of all Japan. How could a farmer identify? We had Pastor Gerald Martin assigned as the preacher, Billy Hilbun the musician, J. B. Bumgardner of Houston and another layman from Houston, together with Woodrow as the laymen. I said to Pastor Nabekura, "You are the pastor, and I will do as you say, but I encourage you to keep him; I am sure you will not regret it." He agreed, and Woodrow found himself in that little church, slipping off his cowboy boots at the entrance, and sliding his stocking feet across the *tatami* floor as he moved up to the front to share his testimony through an interpreter.

I was not present, but I heard from team members and others what took place when he gave his testimony. The same compassion and warmth that I had felt so many times back in our little Texas church were being released on that small church. As he looked out from the pulpit into the hearts and eyes of the Japanese, realizing that many of those present had not yet heard the story of Christ, his heart broke with compassion, and the tears streamed down his cheeks as he shared, through his interpreter, what Christ meant to him.

I would never want to say that a layman or a visitor for one week in a country is more effective than a missionary, but I have to say that I think I have never been more effective in my missionary career than was that farmer in presenting the gospel in that campaign. Missionaries can do some things that the farmer could not do; but I could not, nor could any missionary, ever do what that farmer did in that pulpit in those days. No two-week participant, no matter how committed, can take the place of the truly committed, hot-hearted, full-time witness. Nor can any hot-hearted, loving, dedicated missionary ever take the place of the dedicated layman and preacher who comes to share even for one week in his country. There is a tremendous need for *all of us* to do *all we can do in God's power.* To attempt the job without both missionary and lay volunteer would be to tie one arm behind our backs and say we were going to win a world without using the tools and the materials God has provided. The people are available. God's people will volunteer. They are effective, and the world will listen to them as they share. To use or not to use all of God's people is no longer an option to be considered; it is now a plan that must be included in any effective worldwide witnessing effort.

On one evening after Woodrow shared his testimony, during the invitation Pastor Nabekura's eighty-two-year-old mother, along with others, came forward trusting Christ as Savior. The pastor was so overcome with joy that he rushed out of the building and into the street rather than let his emotional, tear-stained face be seen by his congregation. This left the team without an interpreter. The congregation sang without being able to express themselves in any other way. Finally the pastor came in, and Woodrow put his arm around him and said, "You need not be ashamed; continue to press the invitation." God blessed and additional victories were witnessed.

I have shared this testimony of Woodrow hundreds of times, and it has been used to encourage thousands of people to go and share their faith overseas. I have shared Woodrow's testimony with every Baptist convention leader I have met in the more than fifty countries where we have gone. All of those leaders quickly recognized God's leading in Partnership through that testimony, and in every case teams of God's people from the United States were invited to come and share in their country! Thank the Lord for all who go and have gone. I am especially glad that we could share our farmer with the people of Japan.

As the teams were leaving the Tokyo airport to return to the United States, I saw that many Japanese Christians had come to say thank you and good-bye to our teams. They showed genuine love and gratitude as they whispered their thanks to each of the team members. But I will never forget the way that little Shinagawa church group expressed their thanks to Woodrow. I saw them hold on to his arm and his clothes and weep like babies as they said good-bye and thanked him for coming. That was a very special demonstration of love after just one week of service together. From that day until this, I have been able to call, challenge, and urge every Christian I meet to give the Lord a chance to use him in world witnessing! I know God can use anyone who has a desire and a love for the Lord.

Alton and Bobbie Ammons

Alton Ammons was a letter carrier in Lubbock, Texas, when he read the call for help in the *Baptist Standard,* calling on all to help in the first large Partnership in Japan in 1963. He decided to send seventeen hundred dollars to the Baptist General Convention of Texas to pay the way for someone else to go. Wade Freeman, in his wisdom and being led of the Lord, wrote back to say, "Mr. Ammons, we don't need your money; we need *you!*"

That was the beginning. Alton had been in the U.S. Navy during World War II and had seen many of his friends killed during the bombing of a Navy ship on which he was serving. He had developed a deep animosity toward the Japanese and had no desire to go to Japan himself. Nevertheless, he felt he could and should provide the money for someone else to go. However, after much prayer, Alton accepted the challenge Dr. Freeman had given and found himself in Japan. His participation provided one of our greatest testimonies of God's power and presence through a team member. Alton and Bobbie Ammons later participated in at least a dozen partnership campaigns from 1963 until the late 1980s.

They now live in Lubbock and are not able to travel because of ill health, but are still a wonderful inspiration to all who go.

With Alton, a retired mail carrier, his family never had sufficient funds to go, but as an example of their commitment, for one of the campaigns, Alton went to the president of the American State Bank in Lubbock, and said, "I would like to borrow some money for a new car, but I don't want the car." The bank president said, "I don't understand." Alton explained, "Normally I would buy a new car at this time, but I don't want the money for that. I want to participate in an evangelistic crusade, and I want the money for *that.*" The president told him he would have to clear that with the bank's directors, and he did! Thus they were able to go!

On another occasion Alton went back to the bank with a similar proposition. He said, "We were planning to buy carpet for our house, but we would like to use the money for a Partnership." Again it was approved, and again they went. On another occasion, they sold their home in order to participate in a crusade. Everything that Alton and Bobbie had was dedicated to the Lord for sharing Christ around the world. They served overseas for a full year on two occasions, witnessing in Japan. In their late years, in poor health, they found themselves without a home but still with great confidence and trust in the Lord.

Two years ago Doris and I opened a letter from Alton and Bobbie. It contained a check for over four thousand dollars as a contribution to Partnership Evangelism! I could not believe my eyes. I knew they had no money. I called immediately to ask what had happened. He said, "A relative has passed away and left a great sum of money to us, and we wanted to use some of it to thank you for letting us be a part of Partnership Evangelism." He also said that the gift to them had provided enough money for them to buy a beautiful two-bedroom condominium very near their church, and he added, "We have found that the amount we received equaled almost to the penny the amount that we have spent participating in all our Partnership campaigns!"

God does not promise to do for everyone just as He did for Alton and Bobbie, but He does promise to take care of every person who gives Him first place in his life. As my Texas translation reads, "Seek ye first the kingdom of God, and I guarantee you, I will take care of all the other details." It *was* true. It *is* true. It *will be* true.

VICTORY REPORTS

THE BEST POSSIBLE WAY to understand what God did in the New Life Movement in Japan in 1963 is to listen to the participants as they tell what God did in their lives and in the churches and cities where they served. It was truly a Holy Spirit-led and empowered campaign!

Mr. and Mrs. Kermit Albertson, Amarillo, Texas—
Sasebo and Ashiya, Japan

The one thing that stands out above all else in our Japan experiences is that it was so obviously God, not men, who made the New Life Movement so successful. We heard no eloquence, nor did we witness any dynamic or clever presentation of the gospel. The testimonies and preaching seemed dull and almost endless through an interpreter. But there was nothing dull about the invitation. The gospel was preached, God was there, and people came forward. It was the most thrilling thing we have ever witnessed. God's power was certainly very evident in Japan.

Chapter 10

Strauss Atkinson, Postman, St. Petersburg, Florida—
Tomino, Japan, and Karita, Taiwan

What impressed me most in the New Life Movement in the Orient was the moving power of the Holy Spirit in all of our meetings and the spiritual hunger of the people. Whether we were in Japan or Taiwan, each time we preached, people were saved. Never did we give an invitation without people confessing Christ as Lord.

J. T. Ayers, First Baptist Church, Brownwood, Texas—
Kochi, Japan

The Baptist Church of Kochi had eleven members. There were forty-four decisions made during the week, twenty-nine conversions, and fifteen seekers.

L. D. Ball, Pastor, Pleasant Grove Baptist Church, Dallas, Texas—
Yahatahama

In the New Life Movement, I am persuaded to believe that:

The Christian religion was dignified.

Churches were edified.

Team members were gratified.

Expenses were justified.

Spiritual blessings were multiplied.

Many hearts were satisfied.

The devil's servants were mystified.

The devil was horrified.

Christ was magnified.

God was glorified.

Reverend and Mrs. Bob Clements, Austin, Texas—
Kagoshima—Tokyo, Taipei, Hong Kong

Never before have we felt more the abiding presence of God's power directing and leading us in all that we did, and in going with us wherever we went. If we had but one request, it would be for God to do it again, not only in the Orient but also in every nook and corner of this world, until Jesus comes again.

Gene L. Combs, Midland, Texas—
Misawa, Osaka, and Higashiyama

"To God be the glory, great things He hath done." In the girls' school in Osaka, over two thousand girls were present. After a brief sermon by Dr. Freeman and because of the power of the Holy Spirit, over twelve hundred girls made professions of faith. It was the greatest thrill of my life to see these girls come forward asking Jesus to come into their hearts.

Vernon O. Elmore, Pastor, Baptist Temple, San Antonio, Texas—
Hamamatsu, Japan

My experience in the New Life Movement was a revelation to me of how God honors faith and uses the witness of willing servants, laboring under severe handicaps. I felt that we were working under New Testament circumstances, reliving the Book of Acts.

W. Herschel Ford, Pastor, First Baptist Church, El Paso, Texas—
Yokohama

I truly believe that the Japan Baptist New Life Movement was one of the greatest Christian endeavors since New Testament days. I believe that from this time on the Japanese pastors will see the advantage of preaching simple evangelistic sermons and giving an invitation for people to accept Christ.

*Thomas H. Frier, Newspaper Executive, Douglas, Georgia—
Aomori, Japan*

At the end of the week when the good-byes were being said, tears streamed down the faces of all the New Life team and every member of the congregation. An influential newspaper editor who had only three months prior become a member of the church after seven years of seeking said, "I have learned more this week than I had learned all my years of study and search put together." He brought a number of the city's leading businessmen to the church during the week, and several made statements of interest in seeking the truth. One elderly lady stood in tears and stated, "I feel as if I were awakening from a deep sleep."

Thank God for the privilege of being a small part of this great evangelistic effort. As we were leaving for the airport, a woman said through our interpreter, "I cannot speak your language, but I can read the love in your eyes."

A. L. Pete Gillespie, Missionary, Osaka, Japan

Five Impressions of the New Life Movement Crusade:

Impression #1: That mass evangelism is certainly one important method of evangelism we must regularly use in Japan.

Impression #2: The Japanese people will respond to a well-planned and well-executed presentation of the gospel. Many took time off from work in order to take part. Our laymen need only the challenge of a big task to perform.

Impression #3: That shorter or one-term appointments by our Foreign Mission Board could be a productive venture. The New Life Movement team members proved this by the vast help they were able to give in only a few short days, even with the difficulties of communication and culture.

Impression #4: That Christian centers built around a church are in order for our large cities. Such centers can afford the opportunity for a continuous program like the New Life Movement and would help in holding many of the community leaders reached through the New Life Movement teams. Very few of our current church units afford this type of facility.

Impression #5: The most pressing need in Japan is for mass evangelism! There is a place for personal work in the initiation of witnessing, and much of this was done in preparation for the New Life Movement; but it is this writer's opinion that in Japanese society, the original approach is best made in a mass meeting with the follow-up being done personally.

Billy Hilbun, Dallas, Texas—
Hirao Baptist Church, Fukuoka

One lady in her testimony told us that she had lived in San Francisco for thirty years and no one had ever told her about Jesus. She had gone back to Japan to live out her remaining years, and thanks be to God, through the New Life Movement, she heard the gospel of Christ and came to know Him as her personal Savior.

Elroy Holt, Layman, Granbury, Texas—
Asahigawa and Obihiro Baptist Churches

The thing most impressed upon me by these crusades is man's utter helplessness and God's power. My prayer is that we will be able to see this in our churches here at home.

The blessings we received from the crusade cannot be put into words. I thank God that I was privileged to have a small part in this great movement of the Holy Spirit, and I pray for our churches here at home.

Truett L. Huffstutler, Hillcrest Baptist Church, Dallas—
Tokyo and Matsue

I am not able to put into words the feelings of my heart concerning the New Life Movement. I had some of the most glorious spiritual experiences of my life. I shall be eternally grateful to the Lord for allowing me to see, hear, and feel His workings in the hearts of the Japanese people.

Robert P. Jackson, Bangs, Texas—
Bonuan First Baptist Church, Philippines

This was without a doubt the most wonderful and rewarding experience of my entire life.

Six observations about the Philippine New Life Movement:

1. The simple gospel is powerful.
2. The personality of the one presenting the simple gospel was of little importance.
3. The only thing we could talk about was Jesus Christ and the plan of salvation in the simplest of terms. And it worked!
4. The missionaries whom I met have tremendous dedication.
5. The miraculous working of God was evident.
6. Evidence of the mighty power of prayer was unmistakable.

I would like to make two suggestions which came to me out of the Philippine Baptist New Life Movement. First, I recommend that we as Southern Baptists adopt this as a new method of missions to be used to complement the already existing mission methods. Second, I recommend that we seek out areas that are ripe and ready for harvest and go there and *stay* until the harvest is finished. We need also to *stay* or send others to help the nationals conserve the harvest.

Edgar Jones, Pastor, Perryton, Texas—
Shinmori Shoji Church, Osaka, Japan

This was the greatest revival experience I have ever felt. I am convinced that this movement was inspired and empowered by the Holy Spirit. In the revival at the Shinmori Shoji church in Osaka, every obstacle fell before the movement of the Holy Spirit. There was no doubt that the Lord was in full control.

Tom Joseph, President, Farmers State Bank, Round Rock, Texas—
Takamatsu, Japan

I hope that Texas Baptists will be doing this same program again in the near future.

Clifford Leddy, Leddy Boot Company, Abilene, Texas—
Obihiro and Same, Japan

The power, boldness, and courage that fell upon us during our team prayers was beyond our comprehension. The compassionate burden placed upon my heart for one boy, girl, man, or woman and the thrill of seeing them accept Christ made me humble and ashamed of my own life. Who can describe it by words, length or breadth, depth or height?

F. A. McMicken, Alvin, Texas—
Seinan Jo Gakuin Junior College, Kokura, Japan

It was wonderful to be in Japan and participate in the New Life Movement. This is a way we can reach people faster for our Lord Jesus Christ. I hope to see this kind of movement continue throughout the world. This effort has proven what God can and will do when we depend on Him. My experience in the movement has increased my faith and led me to depend more fully upon Him to fulfill His promises found in the Bible.

Charles B. Mahaffey, Oil Business, Tomball, Texas—
Kumamoto and Yokkaichi, Japan

As a layman, I have never seen the Holy Spirit so active in the hearts of men. It was evident in every meeting. When the Christians of Japan and Texas called upon the Lord, He responded by giving us the greatest evangelism program of the century. The experiences I had in Kumamoto and Yokkaichi with God and the Japanese people have transformed me into a witness for Him in the United States!

James R. Maples, Evangelist, Texas City, Texas—
Asaka and Asakusa, Japan

Never have I been more aware of the power of the Holy Spirit.

Elson E. Marks, Houston, Texas—Hitachi Mission, Japan

If I live to be a thousand years old, I will remember this experience as if it were yesterday! We prayed earnestly that through the power of the Holy Spirit we would see the nine members in Hitachi Baptist Mission increase to at least eighteen. The first meeting in the city auditorium was the first time I had shed tears for lost souls in many years. We had sixteen decisions—eleven professions of faith and five seekers. We had a total of thirty-five professions of faith and thirteen seekers.

J. W. Miller, Businessman, Midland, Texas—
Higashiyama Baptist Church, Japan

The New Life Movement represented to me the greatest thrill of my Christian life, except for my own conversion experience.

I went to Japan with considerable misgivings about what a not-very-effective layman could do. It is plain to me now that the Holy Spirit will honor any effort that is bathed in concern and prayer, no matter how clumsy the human instrument. I have often wondered why we so seldom see outpourings of the Holy Spirit like the first-century church experienced. Praise God, I saw just such a manifestation in Japan! The Comforter was so near on occasions that He was as real to me as my own family! We found an unspeakable bond of Christian love that united brothers and sisters in Christ everywhere, regardless of language barriers. We saw a tiny mission of five members (three of them the pastor and his family) register one hundred and forty decisions in a five-day meeting. We saw God's miracle of grace work in the hearts of people that had never heard the gospel before. We fellowshipped with spiritual giants, saw faith honored, and saw God's precious promises claimed.

If I live and God is willing, I want to go back to Japan as often as I can to serve in any way I can. I want to enlist other laymen in a continuing program of some kind. I earnestly pray that God will continue to give us, as American Christians, the vision and the faith to attempt great things in the name of our precious Redeemer.

Lester Probst, Evangelist, First Baptist Church, Coleman, Texas— Nakama Baptist Church, Japan

Words cannot describe what I experienced in Japan. The great power of the Holy Spirit was manifested in every service. I have never been in such services as those 6:00 A.M. prayer services in Nakama. Many times back in my room at the inn, I actually fell on my face before God and felt I would die if God didn't save souls in Japan. I had prayed for a burden, but I never realized the price I would pay when God answered. At the first evangelistic service, seventy-two young people jammed into the little church—many of them standing. When I gave the invitation, forty-two accepted Christ as Savior. From Thursday through Sunday, more than two hundred decisions were made.

On the first Sunday back in Coleman, I said, "If I were young enough to be approved by the Foreign Mission Board, I would go back to Japan as a missionary." The next Sunday my older daughter, Rhonda Kay, fourteen years of age, came out of the choir and said, "Daddy, God is calling me to be a missionary. I believe it is to go to Japan." I didn't tell her that some of the people in Nakama had seen her picture and said, "Maybe she will come to Japan some day as a missionary." I want to go back to Japan myself!

H. F. "Hank" Scott, Pastor, First Baptist Church, Wilson, Texas— Tokyo and Sapporo, Japan

We went to Japan knowing that we would face many difficulties, but one thing we knew was that this was God's assignment for us, and for our people who remained at home, God's assignment was to pray without ceasing.

I must confess that I did not expect to see such a demonstration of God's power. I still thrill as I recall that day after day and night after night we witnessed the power of God in the meetings in Tokyo and then in Sapporo. This makes me know without any doubt that this can happen in any nation in the world today. It only depends on the desire and the faith of God's people to see it realized.

Another unforgettable experience occurred on the afternoon of the final big meeting in the sports center in Sapporo. A Japanese man came to that afternoon service and was the first person to step out and receive Christ as Savior. This was the first time that man had ever been in a church or attended any kind of a religious meeting. He came as the direct result of the University Cowboy Band. He heard the band playing on the roof garden of a large department store, where he heard the announcement that the band would play that night in the sports center. He attended that night and there met Pastor Tomita, who had invited him to the afternoon service. The man accepted Christ as Savior. He is a Christian today because of this group of dedicated young men from Hardin-Simmons University who attracted his attention, as was the case with many, many people in Japan who found Christ as Lord. We nicknamed him Smiley because from the time he trusted Jesus until the last time we saw him, he had a broad smile on his face and a longing to share what Christ had done for him.

Joe B. Smith, Fort Worth, Texas—Asaka Baptist Church, Japan

It is my belief that the New Life Movement is and has been an overwhelming indication of God's power at work in Asia. I believe that the one key answer to the success of the movement is the prayer *with faith* of the Christians around the world. This must be viewed as only the beginning! This can become a pattern of evangelism around the world. God's Holy Spirit has dealt with the people of Japan in a very wonderful and powerful way. I firmly believe that God is challenging Southern Baptists around the world to rise up and claim the world for Him.

H. Bailey Stone, Jr., Pastor, First Baptist Church, McKinney, Texas—Ichikawa, Japan

The story of Ichikawa will always live in my heart as one of the greatest experiences of my life. I have the confidence that "He who hath begun a good work in them will perform it until the day of Jesus Christ."

Marvel G. Upton, Pastor, Sunray, Texas—
Misawa Baptist Church, Japan

I have been praying for twenty years for God to do in America just what He did in the New Life Movement in Japan. I believe God is moving in a mighty way and that it would be foolish to believe anything in the proportions of the Japan Movement would cease in a matter of a short time. I am praying that God will move in America the way He has in Japan. This Japan experience can be described only as the *mighty hand of God in action!*

Avery Willis, Jr., Pastor, Grand Prairie, Texas—
Fukui Baptist Mission

(Dr. Willis is presently senior vice president for overseas operations for the International Mission Board.)

During the New Life Movement in Japan, I served as the preacher for the team in Fukui City. We saw a mighty demonstration of the power of the Holy Spirit when 234 persons made professions of faith in Christ, plus numerous other decisions. On Wednesday night we met in a little mission. It was overflowing with ninety-one people present. The Holy Spirit's presence was felt, and when the invitation began, one person finally came, but before she could reach the front of the building, she was followed by many more. Forty-five persons out of ninety-one came to accept Christ as Savior, all of them first-time decisions.

On Saturday we spoke to the English-Speaking Society at Fukui University. At the conclusion of my message, I said, "Since I do not know your rules, I suppose it will be all right if I break them." I then asked them to commit themselves to Christ. Among those responding was the English professor who had organized the society. He came to the church service the next morning and publicly professed his faith in Christ during the invitation.

We spent two days in the town of No, which has a population of fifty thousand people and only three Christians. . . . The Fukui Mission wanted to begin a church there, but it had only twenty-eight members when the New Life Movement began and now has over two hundred members to disciple. Who will go over and help them?

Robert L. Lee, Executive Secretary, Louisiana Baptist Convention

The Japan evangelistic effort proved to be the highest spiritual moment of our lives.

Shuichi Matsumura, Campaign Director

We were impressed again with 1 Corinthians 2:4: "My speech and my preaching is not with enticing words of men's wisdom, but in demonstration of spirit and power."

The messages and testimonies were simple and brief, but many people responded and found Christ as Lord. Some pastors are now saying we need to reexamine our thoughts on evangelism and on our messages. The New Life Movement has given our pastors a new confidence and an optimistic outlook for the future. Like dynamite, the New Life Movement blasted off the predominant negativism in the Japanese churches and among Japanese pastors. They have baptized more people in the past two months than in the previous year.

Japanese pastors have learned the importance of the invitation. Prior to the New Life Movement, there was hardly a church in Japan that gave an invitation. We have learned that it is a must for us to challenge our people to receive Christ in every service.

Dr. Matsumura concluded by saying, "'Except the Lord builds the house, they labor in vain that build it.' We planned the best we could, and we labored to the maximum of our human strength. God accomplished the mighty work. William Carey said, 'Attempt great things for God; expect great things from God.' This was dramatically illustrated in the New Life Movement."

W. H. "Dub" Jackson, Campaign Codirector

The New Life Movement took place before it became acceptable to use "ordinary Christians" overseas and was used to open the door for future generations to become witnesses around the world. It helped to demonstrate to the church what the Lord could do and wanted to do in world witnessing. We saw again that the message was more important than the messenger.

In 1963, over a period of six weeks, 549 volunteers traveled to Japan and Asia sharing their love for Christ, and approximately 45,000 Asians came forward inviting Christ into their lives. That kind of response in a Buddhist and Shinto environment caused every Christian to rejoice and know that God is still *able*, even in our day! All who participated came away saying, "This was of God, and it *must* continue."

I came away from that experience with two strong convictions.

1. Any Christian who loves the Lord with all of his heart, knows the plan of salvation, and has a desire to see others receive Christ as Lord can be effective anywhere in the world.

2. Christians from all walks of life *must assume* a more direct and *personal responsibility* for sharing their own personal testimony with the world.

OPEN DOORS—DECISION TIME!

I WAS EXCITED ABOUT WHAT HAD HAPPENED and about what was going to happen as these 150 teams spread out across Japan, but what were we going to do after that! One of the most frustrating experiences I have ever had came when I learned we were not planning to do it again soon.

I kept asking, "Why are we not planning to come back and follow up with similar armies of God's people?" I believe to this day Satan's walls of materialism would have fallen in Japan and Japan would have become one of the great Christian nations of the world had we continued in faith until the Lord had given total victory! It goes back again to those simple words of Jesus: "According to your faith be it done unto you," and, "Ask and ye shall receive." What are we asking for? A one-time demonstration of God's power or *total victory?*

Throughout the excitement and victory that God gave during the New Life Movement, the Lord was giving me a vision of what *could happen if we could mobilize* God's people for world evangelism. The Japanese requested another partnership campaign, but the next year came, and no partnership. Then yet another year, and still no partnership! Southern Baptists had no plan that would let the total church become involved in sharing Christ around the world.

K. Owen White was pastor of First Baptist Church, Houston, and president of the Southern Baptist Convention, one of our best-loved pastors and a great friend. Once he said, "Dub, one of the hardest things for me is to find and know God's will!" I did not understand him then, but as we returned to the United States seeking His will concerning the place to launch Partnership Evangelism, we came to understand what he was saying.

Doris and I became almost frantic as we waited and wondered how long it would be before Southern Baptists would start moving again in partnership. We wrote many letters and met many Baptist leaders on the mission field and from the United States, but there seemed to be no movement toward using all our people in world missions.

In the midst of this prayer and searching, we received a letter from Dr. White, inviting me to become his associate pastor at First Baptist Church. I knew he was committed to finding a way to involve all Southern Baptists in a New Life Movement kind of evangelism all over the world. After agonizing over leaving Japan, we replied to Dr. White and to our mission in a letter explaining to them that we would return home to seek the help we knew we would need if Partnership ever became a reality!

We resigned from the Foreign Mission Board and accepted the position with Dr. White in Houston and began the long pilgrimage toward seeing Partnership Evangelism become a reality.

We spent a joyous year praying and sharing our burden while at Houston, and many people assured us that help was on the way. After our year with Dr. White in Houston, as we had originally planned, we called the Foreign Mission Board and asked for permission to return to Japan to wait for the flood of laypeople that we were now sure would soon be coming to help. We gained much from having that one year with Dr. White and the wonderful people of First Baptist Church. That encouraging time reconfirmed to us that our people at home were willing and ready to accept any challenge, anywhere in the world, if we would only call on them. Deacon Joe Hugghins and his wife Beverly, of that church, were typical of the dedicated laypeople who filled our churches and wanted to help. Joe later served thirteen years as a lay member of the World Evangelism Foundation's executive committee, which, along with the overseas advisory board, guided every action of the World Evangelism Foundation.

After the year with Dr. White and many meetings and conferences with Baptist leaders who also wanted to see the total church included in the overseas mission program, we decided that it was time to return to Japan. Just before returning, I met Paul Stephens, director of the Southern Baptist Radio and Television Commission, who said, "Dub, would you be willing to serve as the coordinator for Asia for the Radio and Television Commission, making sure that our Christian programs are presented by radio and television across that part of the world?" He said we would, together, seek to see every Asian TV antenna become a receiving board for the gospel of Jesus Christ! Dr. Stephens was a man of vision, and I immediately saw how his plan and his vision could make a difference. I had come to believe that the Foreign Mission Board and Southern Baptists were now ready to cooperate in a program that would include the total church. I thought that this might be another way of reaching even more people with the gospel. What a challenge!

I was never happier than when we went to Fort Worth to meet Paul and accept his invitation. I am eternally grateful to him for his trust and faith in me and his willingness to let me be his director for Asia. But as Doris and I prayed, God did not give us permission to accept that challenge. It seemed that we were supposed to go back to Japan.

As we prepared to return we received some confusing letters from the Japan mission, seemingly indicating that if we returned, we would have to give up our plan for mass evangelism and be willing to go out to one of the rural areas of the country to serve. Our response to the mission was lengthy, but one sentence is sufficient to summarize the reply. "We are willing to go anywhere, but we would never go anywhere we had to pledge to give up our hopes for mass evangelism." Thank the Lord the Japanese leaders were reassuring and expressed a strong desire for Doris and me to come back and serve with them. When we returned, they elected me to serve as the associate director of evangelism for the Japan Baptist Convention and encouraged us in every way to keep on aggressively seeking to see Japan come to know the Lord!

Working with Pastor Kawaguchi, the evangelism director, we made plans for two Partnership campaigns to take place in 1966 and 1967. It was a help, but it still was not all the Lord wanted done. We had thought that by this time, great hosts of people would be coming to help. Japan was not quite as open as it had been in 1963. There was beginning to be a wave of opposition to evangelism and to Americans. Our primary concern, however, was not with the circumstances in Japan but with the response of Southern Baptists. We knew they did not see the need and opportunities here as we did, or they would have responded. Again, Doris and I were faced with a decision: Should we give up on the idea of Partnership Evangelism, or should we go back and try again until the people at home came to understand that missions is all of us working together at home and overseas?

Winfred Moore, pastor of First Baptist Church, Amarillo, Texas, had a vision for Partnership and sent a letter inviting us to come and join his staff and coordinate Partnership for their church. I thought that if we could see that great church lead out in Partnership, it would encourage many other churches at home and would be the beginning of what we had felt God wanted done. I would have gladly gone, but the deacons decided not to try it. We were faced again with the decision, What shall we do, and how shall we do it? Should we wait, or should we go to share the message of the *urgency* of Partnership to be done *now?*

If I have any talent at all, it is not in the area of waiting. My son Bill once said to me, "Dad, patience is not one of your spiritual gifts." He was exactly right. I have always had a deep conviction that if God wants something done, we need to do it *now.* I recently read a prayer that said, "Lord, Give me your patience and give it to me *now!*" I am afraid that was how I prayed.

Billy Graham Crusade, Tokyo

While still in Japan in 1967, the Lord gave me the tremendous joy and opportunity of serving as cochairman, together with Hatori Sensei, of the 1967 Billy Graham Tokyo Crusade. I also worked that year as an associate with Dan Piatt, the overseas crusade coordinator for the Graham organization. Our Southern Baptist Foreign Mission Board granted Dr. Graham's request that I be placed on a leave of absence to work with them for one year in that crusade, and it was a full year of hard work and joy! God blessed the campaign, as He always does with Dr. Graham. He blessed all of us, and many came to receive Christ as Lord. At the close of the campaign, as I drove Dr. Graham and T. W. Wilson back to Haneda Airport for their return flight, I shared again with them my concern and burden for all Southern Baptists to become involved directly in missions with more than just their giving. Dr. Graham said, "Before you resign, be sure to contact me."

We were deeply grateful for Dr. Graham's interest, and I did talk with them, but there was no plan for Dr. Graham to add the Partnership kind of program to his regular campaigns. God was blessing in the usual great way in his campaigns, and there was certainly no need to consider adding or taking away anything from such a victorious program.

Bob Pearce and World Vision

Still praying about returning to the United States to set up our own organization, I met with one of my heroes of the faith, Bob Pearce, founder and president of World Vision. I do not think I have ever met a man with more faith than Dr. Pearce. In the midst of our struggle to find God's will, Dr. Pearce invited us to join with him and carry out Partnership Evangelism through his great organization. He agreed to everything we proposed and said his organization would give us full support in seeing to it that Partnership became a reality. I was prepared to join with him when he became ill and shortly thereafter left World Vision. I wondered, *Would we ever be able to do what we felt God wanted us to do?* Again the door for starting Partnership had closed.

Another Open Door?

Just as we had decided to resign and start our own Partnership organization, John Haggai, one of the finest evangelists I have ever heard, came to Tokyo to visit us. In our discussions John offered to sponsor Partnership through his organization. In reading his book *How to Win Over Worry*, I felt I had found a man who had exactly the same vision that God had given to us. We made plans to join with him, even arranging details and discussing salaries; but at the last minute I could not have a clear leading from the Lord to join with them. I was disappointed! I had to tell him we felt we had to keep on until we could see our denomination committed to Partnership.

I must say here that I have never felt that Partnership could only be done through my own denomination, but I had a strong desire to see Southern Baptists included in Partnership. I think some of my most encouraging and joyous experiences had come to me through organizations such as Youth for Christ, Billy Graham Evangelistic Association, World Vision, and the Far East Gospel Crusade.

Encouragement from Bill Bright

In the midst of the many negatives and refusals concerning the use of laymen in world evangelism, I met Bill Bright, founder and president of Campus Crusades for Christ International. We met in the Adolphus Hotel in Dallas, and Dr. Bright encouraged me to keep on until Partnership Evangelism became a reality. I even felt that God was willing to see Partnership Evangelism become a part of their great organization. Certainly no other man ever had more confidence in using and mobilizing the ordinary person for world witnessing than Dr. Bright. I thank God for his timely encouragement. He is certainly one of the most faithful men of vision and courage that God ever gave to our world.

God Shows the Way

Gerald Martin, one of my dearest friends, at that time serving as president of the Southern Baptist Pastor's Conference, urged us to come back to the United States and set up a base for

Partnership Evangelism. He invited me to speak at the Southern Baptist Pastor's Conference, and while I was there, he suggested to Leo Eddleman, president of New Orleans Baptist Theological Seminary, that I join his staff as assistant to the president to kick off a program of Partnership. In a conference with Dr. Eddleman, we decided that we would return to the United States as his assistant and establish what would be called the World Evangelism and Research Center. What a joy it was to find a Southern Baptist organization and leader who was willing to let me be a part of his ministry and allow us to pursue the vision God had given! We returned to the United States and to New Orleans in 1968, to begin working on what appeared to be an impossible dream.

We returned with a strong conviction that if we were ever to see Partnership Evangelism become a reality, someone would have to give themselves full-time to that goal. Dr. Eddleman gave us an office and an excellent secretary, Dorothy Patterson, wife of Dr. Paige Patterson. She was so talented that I really felt like I was her secretary. She was invaluable in those early days. We moved to New Orleans, built a home, and prepared to let that be our base for years to come. But ill health forced Dr. Eddleman to resign a year later, and that meant I, too, had to resign. We were again faced with the challenge of finding a base and place for Partnership. The thought came to me that maybe we should just go back to Japan, where we had enjoyed our work so much, and pray that someone else would lead until Southern Baptists accepted Partnership.

Decision Time Again

If we returned to Japan, we would have the opportunity of preaching the gospel every Sunday to a congregation where many unsaved people would be present and many decisions could be made. When we had come back to the States in 1968, we had returned believing that was what God wanted us to do. The Foreign Mission Board had been kind to us and had left the door open for our return to Japan. Our prayer was constantly, "Oh, Lord, what would *you* have us do?" Finally we met with Dr. Cauthen and Dr. Crawley at the Capitol Inn Motel in Nashville to pray and discuss our future service. Dr. Cauthen, in his love for missions and his compassion and concern for a world, could easily get through to my heart and cause me to want to go back to Japan. I remember his saying, "Dub, why couldn't you go back and have a campaign in Fukuoka, another one later in Osaka, another one in Nagoya, another one in Tokyo, and another in Hokkaido?" He was right. It could have been done, and I would have loved to do it. It would have been a ministry of great meaning and joy for me and for our family. I asked Cauthen, "If we go back, is the board ready to appoint someone to coordinate a ministry like Partnership Evangelism?" He explained that the board had recently added to its staff and that adding a person for Partnership did not seem to be a possibility at that time.

Since the board could not reassure us that Partnership Evangelism would become one of their priorities, we were again faced with the question: Shall we give up, or shall we keep on until we see the ministry of Partnership Evangelism become a part of our Southern Baptist life? Finally I said to Dr. Cauthen, "I believe that we must stay here and do our best to find a way to see Partnership Evangelism become a way to witness overseas. We will do this, not in opposition to the Foreign Mission Board, but as best we can in *cooperation with* the board. We will try to find a way for Partnership Evangelism to become what we think God expects it to be."

Thus the decision was made. I met with our area secretary, Jim Belote, to let him know we would stay in America and work on Partnership. As we met, I found myself wavering again! In fact my desire to be back in Japan was so strong that I told Dr. Belote, "I just don't see how we can resign. I believe God would have us resign, but I cannot imagine not being a part of witnessing in Japan." Dr. Belote was so kind and said, "Dub, you believe God wants you here to work on Partnership. You should go ahead and do it! Rejoice and move on!" Had Dr. Belote not encouraged us to keep on with our dream, I do believe we would have given up and gone back to Japan that day. I rejoice *now* that we did stay and that Partnership Evangelism has finally become a part of our Southern Baptist worldwide outreach.

Thank God for His leadership and for circumstances that kept us in the States and with the task of Partnership Evangelism until the Lord gave the victory. The goal of seeing Southern Baptists accept Partnership would take another thirteen years of service in the World Evangelism Foundation, an organization the Lord would lead us to establish.

WORLD EVANGELISM FOUNDATION BEGINS

ALL OF US LONGED TO SEE THE DAY when armies of God's people would be going out to share Christ across the world. When I consider the joys that God gave through Partnership Evangelism, I cannot help but look back in wonder and thanksgiving at how many times the Lord kept us pointed toward the goal of Partnership when we were tempted to give up.

Organization

With the resignation of President Eddleman, we chose to move back to Texas and expedite the organization of the World Evangelism Foundation. That was a move into spiritual warfare even more frightening and demanding than the flight into physical combat in World War II! The battles for Partnership were going to demand all of our efforts and God's direction for the next thirteen years. Only God would be able to lead us through. We were leaving the seminary and returning to Texas without salary, and we had lost the Foreign Mission Board college scholarships for our five children, soon to enter college! We had also forfeited most of our future retirement, and had come face-to-face with many new uncertainties. Nevertheless, we had a conviction that this was what God would have us do.

We began by renewing fellowship with some dear friends such as Hank Scott, pastor of Bacon Heights Baptist Church, Lubbock; Gene Hawkins, pastor of First Baptist Church, Seminole, Texas; and Claude Cone, pastor of Calvary Baptist Church, Lubbock.

One of our first actions after moving to Abilene was to call on another friend, L. L. Morris, pastor of First Baptist Church, Midland. He introduced us to one of his members, Evelyn Linebery, and suggested we meet with her concerning possible support. I set up an appointment and asked Hank Scott to go with me, because his father had once been the foreman on her ranch. It is wonderful to see how God puts things together.

I have forgotten the details of our visit, but we knew when we left that God had been with us and that He was blessing. Ultimately, through the generosity of Mrs. Linebery and her foundation over a period of twenty years, God led her to put over $1,100,000 into Partnership Evangelism! No one could have predicted this when the initial contact was made—not even Mrs. Linebery. How we thank God for her! She has gone on to be with the Lord, but she has the eternal gratitude of thousands who have come to know Christ through Partnership.

The official beginning of World Evangelism Foundation was dated October 5, 1970. Our trustees elected the following executive committee: W. H. Jackson, Jr., director; Gene Hawkins, chairman; T. V. Farris, vice chairman; Claude Cone; Carlos McCleod; Robert Gunn, treasurer; H. F Scott, assistant treasurer; L. L. English, auditor; Gerald Martin; Ramsey Pollard, chairman of the

United States advisory board and member of the executive committee; Carl Ballard; Evelyn Linebery; and Frank Gillham.

Our U.S. Advisory Board was composed of Herschel H. Hobbs, Ramsey Pollard, E. Hermond Westmoreland, Clifton Wooley, Herbert Reynolds, Greer Garrett, Bill Tanner, W. H. Souther, Macon Delavan, Jack Hamilton, Joe Hugghins, and Don Berry.

This new World Evangelism Foundation organization was set up in 1968 and reaffirmed in 1970 in board meetings chaired by Ramsey Pollard. From the very beginning we had an overseas advisory board. The first member of this board was Shuichi Matsumura, president of the Japan Baptist Convention, and the one who had been giving direction in the preparation for our first partnership in Japan, even before we left Tokyo in 1968. Later we added over twenty overseas advisory board members in countries where we were to have partnerships.

One of the unique features of the World Evangelism Foundation from its inception was that no decision was made and no action was taken without the approval of the overseas advisory board. Our work was overseas, so we wanted the leading and directions to come from there. The overseas advisory board was no rubber-stamp committee. It provided the wisdom needed to make possible our opportunity to witness worldwide.

God Provides a Staff

Just as all of the needs for Partnership Evangelism were provided, and many in miraculous ways, the World Evangelism Foundation staff was certainly selected under God's leadership. It was one of the best staffs ever assembled to carry out a program of evangelism overseas.

I cannot take credit for selecting these people the Lord gave to us. I am confident that they were His choices. They were called into the task of Partnership Evangelism just as clearly as any missionary or participant before or since.

The first staff member invited to help put World Evangelism Foundation together was Don Maddox, a retired Air Force pilot, a full colonel, and a command pilot with more than thirty-one years of flying and executive experience. Don came from the famous missionary Maddox family and seemed to embody all of the great traits that God had given to that family through the years.

Don and Ruth Maddox joyfully separated from the Air Force and moved to Abilene, Texas, to help assemble an office that was to coordinate more than ten thousand people to share Christ across the world. I have never known anyone anywhere with more diplomacy, love, and ability than Don and Ruth Maddox. We thank God for them.

T. A. Patterson, longtime pastor and former executive secretary of the Baptist General Convention of Texas, together with his wife Roberta (better known as "Honey"), coordinated the New Life Movement in 1963 stateside. Upon his retirement from the Texas Convention, he continued his commitment to world witnessing by serving as executive vice president for World Evangelism Foundation until World Evangelism Foundation turned Partnership over to the Foreign Mission Board in 1981. Dr. "Pat" knew everyone and everyone knew him! He called on all to cooperate in Partnership and was an amazing and faithful leader.

Two of my most beloved friends over the years were missionaries Oscar and Marie Bozeman. They were greatly loved and respected in Korea as missionaries, and Oscar was one of the most effective evangelistic missionaries ever appointed by our board anywhere. It was a sad day in 1999 when we had to say good-bye to him and realize that he was one of the first of the World Evangelism Foundation staff to go on to his reward.

Jerry and Janice Byrd participated as volunteers in the German Partnership of 1973 and joined World Evangelism Foundation from the Air Force to serve as arrangements coordinator. Jerry, at the time of his resignation from the Air Force, was a C–141 airplane commander and a superb pilot and organizer whom God would use in amazing ways to make available the facilities needed to support the program of evangelism overseas. He was able to do almost anything at any time, in record time.

Jim and Mary Humphries were loved and respected missionaries from Vietnam, where Jim was the longtime pastor of Trinity Baptist Church in Saigon. He recognized the urgent need for everyone to witness and reluctantly but joyously joined the staff of World Evangelism Foundation. He sought to enlist American churches and people to participate in sharing Christ with the world.

In the midst of the first World Evangelism Foundation French Partnership, Newman McLarry accepted an invitation to join our World Evangelism Foundation. He was a talented preacher and leader. Both he and his wife Sue were an inspiration in the office and shared the vision of Partnership in many areas throughout Texas and the Southern Baptist Convention. His father-in-law, C. Wade Freeman, was one of the key leaders in the New Life Movement. Newman has also gone on to be with the Lord.

David Bynum was a faithful office worker and a special help in our business office under Don Maddox.

Ben Meith was a longtime member of the World Evangelism Foundation executive committee who had a special burden for

Mexico and South America. Eventually he was led to leave World Evangelism Foundation and start his own witnessing work called International Crusades. Later Ben and his wife Bertha brought their staff from International Crusades and rejoined the staff of World Evangelism Foundation. Ben was a farmer in west Texas when he participated in the first Japan partnership. He never lost the vision of what could happen when an ordinary Christian went out with compassion and shared with the world what Christ meant to him. When World Evangelism Foundation was passed to the Foreign Mission Board, Ben and some of the staff reorganized to carry on Partnership campaigns.

Others who came into the World Evangelism Foundation with International Crusades included Rodney and Debra Cavett, Javier and Sandee Elizondo, Alfred and Christine Richards, Francisco and Rosalva Nunez, and Jim Walters, an Air Force pilot who served as coordinator of arrangements for International Crusades.

Calvin and Juanez Beach were a hot-hearted, loving team that God used in enlisting churches and individual Christians to share their love with the world. Calvin had pastored the First Baptist Church of Plains, Texas, and they had been involved in a marvelous program of witnessing in Korea with miraculous results. He was a constant inspiration and great help as he called on Southern Baptists to go and witness.

No office was ever able to operate effectively without a special office director. This person for World Evangelism Foundation was Dorma Probst, a college classmate of ours and a superb musician. She was a dedicated pastor's wife with a burning vision for missions. Dorma Buchanan married Lester Probst, and served with him until his passing, and was a tremendous office manager when World Evangelism Foundation most needed her. I cannot say enough about Dorma, who was able to coordinate the work of all the secretaries and take care of the many details of seeing World Evangelism Foundation successfully involved in more than one hundred nationwide campaigns.

Billy Sue Easley was an efficient, able secretary who helped Dorma make sure all the activities of our office were efficiently and lovingly carried out. In 1980 Dorma and Billy Sue were promoted to staff positions because of the responsibilities they were carrying in sharing Christ with the world.

Dollie Culp, longtime worker in the Texas Baptist Woman's Missionary Union, was one of the most able expediters and organizers we ever had. She also served as my executive secretary and helped coordinate my activities—if that was ever possible.

First Executive Committee Meeting

The World Evangelism Foundation executive committee was organized at a meeting in the Ming Tree Chinese Restaurant on Slide Road in Lubbock on October 15, 1970. Everything that has taken place since then has been the result of prayer and the miracle-working power of our Lord. Every executive committee meeting of the World Evangelism Foundation was like a revival meeting. God was present in every meeting, and we were aware of His leading. The committee faced many challenges and tremendous difficulties, but it was a joy. We were watching God do His work!

Some Initial Cautions

We did not use the term *missions* or *mission volunteers* in describing World Evangelism Foundation and its work, for those words usually suggested some sort of sacrifice. We disagreed with that picture completely. A person who is called to serve outside the boundaries of the United States in world witnessing is *not* making a sacrifice. When we are serving the Lord in the place He would have us serve, we are in the midst of the greatest *joy* that God can give, not sacrifice! Somehow, we must relay that message to people who are considering God's call to serve around the world. A partner or missionary does not lose anything! It is a battle, a joy, and a victory!

Evelyn Linebery

World Evangelism Foundation was established to make it possible for *everyone* to participate in witnessing. We purposely avoided using the words *help* and *missions.* Instead, we used words like *Christians, sharing,* and *working together.*

World Evangelism Foundation's Goals and Purposes

From the very first days of World Evangelism Foundation, we described our goals and purposes and did everything possible to keep focused in that direction. It was stated as follows:

The goals of World Evangelism Foundation are to:

1. Get the total church involved in world witnessing.
2. Find the most effective ways of reaching the most people with the gospel *now!*
3. Provide encouragement and inspiration for stateside and overseas personnel.
4. Pray and expect many to come to know Christ as Lord.
5. Encourage and inspire every participant and overseas church.

We were known by few, mistrusted by many, and without any visible means of support!

Early Days

Our work always moved forward with the conviction that the only possible hope of sharing the gospel with the world was for the total church to become involved. This conviction was unshakable. Through the fire for many years, no argument, no logic, and no circumstance could short-circuit this conviction or change our direction.

Sources of Encouragement

Although our Convention and the Foreign Mission Board had not yet come to believe in this approach, we had many wonderful leaders who strongly believed that this was of God. These leaders included K. Owen White, Ramsey Pollard, T. A. Patterson, C. Wade Freeman, Herschel Hobbs, J. D. Gray, R. G. Lee, and many others. There were also laymen who were very encouraging, such as Joe Hugghins, First Baptist Church, Houston; Robert Gunn, Calvary Baptist Church, Lubbock; and L. L. English, First Baptist Church, Wichita Falls. Very close pastor friends like G. M. Cole, Ridglea Baptist Church, Fort Worth, and Gerald Martin of Memphis, Tennessee, faithfully encouraged and supported World Evangelism Foundation.

Our children, my wife, and my faithful parents were unwavering in their confidence that God was leading. An interesting illustration of the love and support from family is seen in this poem written by our youngest daughter, Juanita. Uprooted from Japan and often moved, it seemed that everything was being taken away when we were called on to move again, this time from

New Orleans back to Abilene. In tears she prayed and then slipped this poem under our bedroom door very late one night:

Confusion

I live where God leads us
*   And God is my master*
Though often it's hard,
*   And I think it's disaster.*

I'm such a young Christian
*   And I know I have much to learn.*
I should let you make this decision,
*   And ignore my selfish yearn.*
Whatever you decide to do,
*   I know it will be right,*
For I won't mind moving again
*   And won't put up a fight.*

I can always make friends in Abilene,
*   And when the going gets rough,*
I'll remember that God sent you there
*   And He will help me, no matter how tough.*

Juanita Jackson—age fourteen
high school freshman, August, 1969

In addition to the encouragement from family and friends, we had the encouragement that comes from knowing that we were doing what God wanted us to do.

Opposition

The Foreign Mission Board had made clear from the beginning that Partnership was not the direction they felt God was leading Southern Baptists at that time. A number of denominational leaders had already, in the period of our first year in the States, made clear that they could not cooperate freely in a program that was not officially a part of Southern Baptist life. It was evident from the beginning that whatever we did would have to be done without the help and encouragement of the denomination. There would be no encouragement or any support from official sources. An excerpt from a letter from Foreign Mission Board executive Keith Parks illustrates this feeling:

> I admire and respect you and know that you are doing a tremendous amount of good. At the same time I have a responsibility to try to do the work that I am committed to do in the most effective way possible. Whereas I see some value to what you are doing, I am still convinced that the local church on the spot, and the missionaries working in the area, are the key to long lasting results. I am so sorry we disagree on methods, but you will understand it if I stand up for my convictions and try to persuade people to see things the way I am convinced is best in the same way that you seek to enlist support for your viewpoint.

History had shown us how difficult it is to initiate a program outside the official channels and have it become an integral part of the denomination. There was a strong possibility that after participating in such a program outside channels for any length of time, whether the program was successful or not, we would be burning all our bridges so far as the possibility of returning to Japan and missionary service with our board was concerned. To present any program outside the convention structure automatically made one "anti-convention." However, if we sit down and analyze every situation, we do not necessarily come out with the decision and the solution that God has in mind. Had the disciples followed the results of their accurate observations made at the time of the feeding of the five thousand, none would have been fed. The disciples would have sent them all away to find food for themselves.

Had we followed what common sense dictated in founding the World Evangelism Foundation, Partnership Evangelism would never have become a reality.

God gave us some understanding for the position of Dr. Cauthen, Dr. Parks, and our Foreign Mission Board. It was easy to see how they could be anxious and unsure about giving approval for people and finances to be involved in a program that was not yet proven. It was easier for us as a new organization, without a reputation, to make decisions and do Partnership. It had to be difficult for the most successful missionary organization in the history of missions to make such a bold departure. As much as we longed for the approval and the cooperation of the Foreign Mission Board, we could understand *why* they could not immediately place approval on a plan they had not yet seen in action on a long-term basis.

As opposition came, I tried never to argue or to criticize in public. In private and with some of my closest friends, we discussed the problem and our concern. As a board or as the World Evangelism Foundation organization, we never made negative statements in public concerning our Foreign Mission Board or the Southern Baptist Convention. Every statement World Evangelism

Foundation made about the Foreign Mission Board and Southern Baptists was positive. I remembered what Billy Graham had said: "Don't argue. Just serve." We tried to do that.

Those first days of Partnership Evangelism were joyous, difficult, victorious, exciting, frightening, and wonderful! Had I not been a young forty-four-year-old, there would have been absolutely no way for us to have been a part of such an effort. I have been involved in some busy programs in my lifetime and some that were very strenuous and nerve-racking, including those in World War II. But never have I been involved in an effort that was so demanding, time-consuming, and exhausting as was the work of Partnership Evangelism.

After many years and many prayers, we were now ready to coordinate the first Partnership campaign under the World Evangelism Foundation. A historic day! We would finally be going back to Japan after the many invitations they had given to us since 1963.

PARTNERSHIP EVANGELISM AND MORE VICTORIES

THE FIRST PARTNERSHIP carried out by the World Evangelism Foundation was to Japan in 1970. Even before then, we had made a commitment to the Japan Baptist Convention to provide five hundred witnesses. We did not have denominational support or even their understanding, but the cooperation of many west Texas churches made the victory possible.

Morris Cobb, the dedicated missions leader at First Baptist Church in Amarillo, was selected by Pastor Winifred Moore to go with me to Japan for the preparation. We met in San Francisco and traveled to Japan, where we had excellent meetings with the pastors and convention leaders. Since First Baptist Church of Amarillo had the potential for the largest team and Pastor Kodama of the Akatsuka Baptist Church wanted a large team, we assigned Amarillo to work with the Akatsuka church.

Upon returning to America, we entered into an intensive program of preparation with the churches coming together for orientation. The first orientation took place in Amarillo, where Corky Farris and Oscar Bozeman brought inspirational messages and I shared the principles that we would follow in the Partnerships.

Chapter 13

All of the churches and participants came with great expectations and left knowing that God was leading. Monthly preparation meetings were scheduled on the campus of Wayland Baptist College in Plainview, Texas. In some of the meetings, we listened to Japanese leaders through a phone hook-up over the public-address system.

Many miracles and victories associated with God's provision and preparation for the Japan campaign were reported in these meetings. In one of our preparation meetings, a young lady stood and said she was going because her family's decision to use the insurance money just received as a result of her brother's death in Vietnam. Another young girl reported collecting Coke bottles to help pay her way. Her dorm room was almost filled with Coke bottles! A twelve-year-old boy from Calvary Baptist Church in Lubbock said that he had been painting house numbers on the curbs at $1.50 to $2.00 a sign and was saving money for the campaign. He succeeded! This is the way it started! These stories were to be repeated hundreds of times as dedicated team members prepared for the one hundred nationwide campaigns God would let us be a part of in more than fifty countries around the world!

Participants testified in every preparation meeting of how God was working and prayed that He would lead. One evening in the orientation meeting with teams from many distant west Texas churches, God gave a great revival! God's presence and power were so evident that no one wanted to leave. The meeting went on past midnight, when the college president called all the dormitories and released the students to join with them in the auditorium. Prayer and testimonies went on all night as the Lord gave inspiration and information to all preparing to witness in Japan!

The preparation culminated in a campaign that saw more than five hundred American team members from twenty-one churches serve in churches across Japan. The choir of First Baptist Church, Dallas, came and inspired all with their music and witness. This was a happy conclusion to the frightening experience of signing contracts with Northwest Orient Airlines to charter two 165-passenger 707s, when we had no funds in sight and few people committed! God filled every seat on those planes, and the choir arrived on flights directly from Dallas.

We arrived in Japan and proceeded to the Imperial Hotel, eager to begin witnessing. The First Baptist Church of Amarillo had fifty-five team members, one of the largest teams ever to go to a single church overseas. The First Baptist Church of Seminole, under the leadership of Pastor Gene Hawkins, had forty-four team members. God blessed with a wonderful demonstration of love and power as churches in Japan saw hundreds come to receive Christ as Lord. This encouraged churches and resulted in more invitations for World Evangelism Foundation to bring more teams to Asia!

Victories in Japan

Much can be said about Partnership Evangelism; however, the testimonies of the participants will give us the best picture of what God did.

Our team in Sapporo was getting on a hotel elevator when a friendly Japanese airline stewardess greeted them. One team member invited her to the services, where she made her profession of faith. Even a short word of greeting and an invitation on a crowded elevator helped this stewardess find victory in her life.

Another team member from Seminole had been plagued with an alcohol problem until his conversion, just three months before joining the team for the Partnership. He resolved to share his experience and the message of salvation. He found that if he got up early, which was easy because of the time change, he could go to the bakeries where people were making bread. There he would have time and opportunity to witness. He carried his bilingual testimony, a marked bilingual New Testament, and a tract explaining the plan of salvation in Japanese. During that week he witnessed to eighty-four Japanese who prayed to receive Christ as Lord and Savior and signed their names in the back of his Bible. Again the Lord was able to show all of us that He will use anyone willing to share in love and present His plan to those around us!

Victories in Spain

At one World Evangelism Foundation executive board meeting, the decision was made to expand the ministry of partnership. Having recently worked with Billy Graham in the 1967 Tokyo crusade, I asked one of his associates to advise me on the persons I should talk to in Europe. He gave me the names of Mr. Vandenhovel of Portugal and Peter Snyder of Berlin, Germany. I went to Europe, and the meeting with Mr. Vandenhovel was special. He assured me that Portugal would welcome the idea of Partnership in his country.

From Portugal I flew to Madrid, where I met Indy Whitten and Mary Ann Forehand, Baptist missionaries to Spain. I had no intention of presenting Partnership in Spain, since I knew the country was closed to aggressive evangelism. Nevertheless, when they heard what had happened in Japan, I was shocked to hear Indy say, "I want you to present this to the promoter of evangelism for the Spanish Baptist Union, Pastor Juan Rodrigo of First Baptist Church of Madrid." I learned that he was really "Mr. Baptist" in Spain. Frankly, I felt that Indy had not understood, for I was still doubtful that an open, aggressive presentation of the gospel on a nationwide scale would be possible in

Spain. However, we made an appointment, and we all met together the next evening.

Indy and Mary Anne helped me share again the story of Partnership with Pastor Rodrigo. At the close he said, "Yes, we have had and still have some problems, but I do believe if we tried, we could have good results with this kind of evangelism. I have been praying about how to promote evangelism, and, brother, you look like my answer!" I was amazed. It was not my plan. If we had Partnership in Spain, it would be because God had led, not because of our vision. Amazingly enough, the first Partnership in Europe would take place in the least likely place for an aggressive program of evangelism—Spain. God was ready to show us again just what He could do and when and where He could do it!

We pledged to Pastor Rodrigo and the Spanish Baptist Union that we would bring an American church and team for every church in Spain that was willing to cooperate. For a year and a half we worked in preparation for the 1971 Spain-U.S.A. Partnership. The Spanish Baptist Union wholeheartedly cooperated. Two hundred and twenty team members from nineteen American congregations journeyed to Madrid to join with our Spanish brothers and sisters in one of the most joyous and victorious evangelistic efforts we had ever seen. Jose Borras, president of the Baptist seminary, and his wife Esther, and Pastor and Mrs. Juan Rodrigo were some of the most effective overseas coordinators ever in Partnership history.

We decided that we would do everything possible to reach the entire nation of Spain for Christ. We prayed for the Spanish leaders and did not forget the smallest church. One morning Pastor Rodrigo said, "Why don't we invite the Catholic cardinal to be our guest at our welcome banquet at the Melia Castilla Hotel?" I was thrilled to be working with such a man of vision and boldness. With great anticipation we went to the Catholic headquarters in Madrid and asked to see the cardinal. The priest who received us said the cardinal was away visiting the pope in Rome but warmly welcomed us and soon ushered in the cardinal's representative to hear our story. We met in a beautiful, high-ceilinged, tapestry-lined room—a bit intimidating but a perfect setting for what was about to take place. I told the cardinal's representative that over two hundred American Christians had been invited to Spain by the Spanish Baptist Union and that we were greatly honored to be coming. I explained that we wanted to invite the cardinal to come to our welcome banquet and receive a gift to express our joy and thanksgiving for the privilege of visiting and witnessing in Spain. I also explained that we wanted to thank him for the hospitality and the freedom that we were experiencing. After explaining to the cardinal's representative how Partnership worked, I was amazed to hear him say, "I think this is a wonderful plan!"

This was in the early days of Partnership, and most Southern Baptists were not yet in favor of Partnership. Thus I said to the priest, "I cannot believe my ears. I know Baptist pastors in Texas who do not favor this plan, but I am so happy to hear that you will welcome us to share our faith in your land."

The cardinal did send his representative to our banquet, and we had the joy of expressing to him publicly our appreciation for the privilege and freedom we were experiencing in Spain. We gave him a gift of the famous "Bible of the Bear," and, of course, the usual Texas cowboy hat and certificate of honorary citizenship of Texas. We were told several times that evening that this was the first time a Baptist minister and a Catholic priest had ever stood together on the same platform in Spain. It was an amazing and historic event. Many tears of joy were shed by the Spanish Baptist

Christians as they recognized that this event signaled a new freedom for them in evangelism.

The governor of Madrid sent his representative to the banquet, as did United States Ambassador Robert C. Hill, who invited all 220 of our team members to meet him at the embassy the next day and receive a briefing from his staff! Senator John Tower had also sent his good wishes for our group, and Vice President Spiro Agnew had sent a message of encouragement. Indy Whitten called a press conference, and *Time, Newsweek,* Associated Press, and United Press International, along with the Spanish news agencies and television personnel, all came! It was an amazing, first-time media event for Baptists or Protestants!

Although Spanish television was closed to all but Catholics, Pastor Rodrigo and I went to the TV headquarters of the leading government station and took with us the recordings and photographs of our musicians, Willa Dorsey and the Ohman Brothers. Willa Dorsey at that time was the leading Black Christian soloist in America and the Ohman Brothers were the finest Christian trumpet players ever. After seeing the pictures and listening to some of the music, miraculously, the TV staff invited them to sing and play on their top-rated Golden Hour program! They were not permitted to preach, but they were free to play and sing!

Baptists of Spain were thrilled and ran ads in their newspapers all across the country inviting people to "tune in tonight" to hear our Baptist musicians in preparation for the Spain-U.S.A Partnership. In that way God gave national television to us at no cost, when it was usually impossible for Protestants to be on TV at all. God blessed that program in a special way!

Before the television program and in keeping with our desire to share the gospel with everyone, we had asked our American embassy personnel and our representatives to help us set up a meeting with Crown Prince Juan Carlos and Princess Sophia, now the king and queen of Spain. Many months passed and many letters had been exchanged before approval came, just as the Partnership was in progress. We were driven to the Zarzella Palace, together with a photographer from the American embassy, Charles Whitten of the Baptist mission, Jose Borras, president of the seminary, and my beloved friend Juan Rodrigo. At the palace we were met by guards dressed in the ornate uniforms of the early days and ushered into a lavishly decorated room to wait for the crown prince. When the prince came in, we were surprised to see that Princess Sophia was also with him. We had not been told that she would be present.

We immediately expressed our deep appreciation to the prince for the hospitality we were experiencing in Spain and for the joy we as American Christians were having in fellowship with the wonderful Christians of Spain. We presented our gifts, including the famous "Bear Bible," and enjoyed some informal time as

With Jose Borras, president, Spanish Baptist Union Seminary; Princess Sophia and Prince Juan Carlos of Spain (center); and Juan Rodrigo, "Mr. Baptist," Madrid; Charles Whitten, SBC missionary in Spain (right)

the prince tried on his cowboy hat and boots. I told him we would give him the white horse when he came to Texas for a visit!

At this point the prince turned to me and asked, "What is the difference between Baptists and Catholics?" I told him that Jose Borras, who was with us, was one of Europe's leading theologians and a graduate of three seminaries, and I would defer to him to answer his question. Jose Borras had been in preparation for the priesthood before entering the ministry as a Baptist preacher, so he was more than qualified to answer that question. He gave a great testimony to the crown prince and clearly pointed out the differences between Catholics and Baptists. When we were ready to leave, I suggested to the prince that if he ever decided to have a Christian service in the palace, I hoped he would not forget Jose Borras, for he would be willing to help in any way.

In leaving we told Princess Sophia that one of our great Christian singers from America, Willa Dorsey, was going to perform on national television that evening and would be dedicating a song to her. That evening Willa sang "Jesus Loves Me" beautifully in Spanish and dedicated it to Princess Sophia. Two years later Jose Borras wrote saying that he was teaching a Bible class in the University of Madrid, and Princess Sophia was in his class! Is there anything our Lord cannot do?

Great Joy

Juan Luis Rodrigo described the Partnership in Spain in these words: "The believers have been strengthened; the churches have been greatly extended and are now expecting victory. God has opened the doors for religious freedom in Spain, something for which Baptists have been praying for more than one hundred years." They requested another campaign for the following year. Rodrigo continued by saying, "The lessons we have received in stewardship, life dedication, and personal evangelism have been especially good. Because of team evangelism, we are now able to contact high government officials and will reap benefits for years to come. Literature has been distributed, people converted, and all of us grown closer to the Lord through this Partnership."

Pastor Rodrigo described the Partnership Campaign vividly: "Through the years, until Partnership, Spanish Baptists have been like goldfish swimming around in a circle in a bowl. Now that we are free, we are still swimming around in that circle—old habits are hard to break, but we are on our way."

Spanish Baptists Speak

Nella Dean Whitten, Southern Baptist missionary, coordinator for the Partnership. "This was the Lord's time for the New Life Crusade in Spain! I am utterly amazed at the results of the campaign! Many doors have been opened that were never open before."

Jose Borras, president of the Spanish Baptist Union, president of the seminary. "The crusade has been an awakening of the Spanish Baptist churches. It has increased our vision! I am impressed with the simplicity of the testimony the people have come to share."

James Buie, Southern Baptist missionary. "Spanish Christians have been encouraged to do things never attempted before. The blessing has not only been for Spanish Baptists; it has also been for me as a missionary. This week brought me to a new commitment for doing personal evangelism."

Pastor Adolfo Lahoz. "Never have we distributed so many tracts. Never have we had so many new people coming to the church. Never have we had so many new young people. Never have we had so many children in Sunday school. Never have we had so many rededications. Never have we sung in the streets. Never have we had fellowship so beautiful. Never have we felt so much joy. Never have we offered a certificate to the mayor. Never have we experienced such power in prayer. Never have we enjoyed smiles so clean. Never have we cried so much. Never have we had a group of visitors who, upon saying good-bye, left us with such emptiness. There have been more new people in our church in the first five days of the crusade than in all the three preceding years."

The governor of Madrid. As we met with the governor of Madrid to express our gratitude as Americans for the hospitality Madrid had shown, the governor gave me a huge Spanish hug and said, "You are always welcome in Madrid, with all of your people!" He sent his representative to our welcome banquet to assure us of his welcome and to express the hope that the Partnership would be successful. Our meeting with the governor took place on the very site where the Spanish Inquisition had occurred.

Pastor Luis Hombre, Malaga, Spain. "I must say that in my ministry, I have never had a week as happy and as full of joy in Christian fellowship. In every way it was a great blessing from the Lord. This Partnership has produced a phenomenal revival."

Eric Sheinberg, missionary in Spain. "I would recommend wholeheartedly this type of endeavor. I was apprehensive at first but am convinced such meetings are a blessing beyond anything that one can realize."

Spiro T. Agnew, vice president of the United States. "It gives me great pleasure to send greetings to you and the more than two hundred Christian laymen of the Southern Baptist Convention participating in this people-to-people program. The time and talent you are giving to this endeavor brings reward not only to your faith but to all faiths, not only to your country, but to the people of Spain as well. I commend you for this effort."

Layman Charles R. Paramore, Dallas. "I doubt that any amount of preparation or orientation would have prepared us for the blessings that have come from this crusade. Throughout the crusade and the time of preparation we could see the evidence of God's presence. We experienced a new closeness to our Christian brothers, and we have taken so much from Spain and left a part of our hearts there."

Mayor of Lerida, Spain. "Pray for me. I have more faith in the Baptist prayers than I do in Catholic prayers."

Priest who attended the service in Alicante, Spain. "This is the first time I have heard a sermon on Jesus in two years, and it came from a Texas farmer."

Team member in Malaga, Spain. "If heaven is any better than this, I think I would die of joy!"

Mayor of Alicante, Spain. "I thought before that all American young people were hippies, but after seeing these examples, I am convinced I was wrong."

Team member in Vallecas, Spain. "All the money in the world couldn't buy the experiences I have had in Spain during this Partnerhsip!"

Mr. Ullahan, who rode on the train with the team to Alicante and reported in Time *magazine.* "There were 238 of them. They had not come to Spain for the sun; they weren't missionaries. They were Southern Baptist laymen, farmers, mail carriers, and bankers. The truth is that they may move all Spain. A local Baptist pastor, a convert from Catholicism, who remembers clearly the bitterness and discrimination given Protestants, said, 'I have not been so nervous since my wedding day.' In every city the meeting drew hundreds of curious families. Local radio stations broadcast Campaign announcements fourteen times daily. In Cordova five thousand tracts were handed out in one day. On the whole, the crusade proceeded smoothly. One of those making decisions was Felix Martinez, a nun who immediately applied for her passport to the United States. Later, she says, she will return to Spain as a Baptist missionary."

Missionary Mary Ann Forehand. "The Partnership resulted in the first Baptist press conference in the history of Spain. Representatives of Associated Press, United Press, Time-Life, and numerous other agencies were in attendance."

Gerald Martin, president of Hannibal LaGrange College and former pastor of Poplar Avenue Baptist Church, Memphis, Tennessee. "When Poplar Avenue Baptist Church began to participate in New Life Partnership crusades, our annual gifts to missions climbed ten times! Total offerings increased. Individuals grew in the grace of giving."

Pastor Luis Hombre, Malaga, delivering the Convention annual sermon in 1971. "It was the greatest experience that we've ever had!"

Srate Tejerina, member of the Spanish Baptist Union. "This is one of the greatest things that Mona Nova Baptist Church has ever had."

Pastor Jose Ortega, First Baptist Church, Valencia. "We had more wonderful experiences in this one week than in all the time of the existence of our church. We had great victories. Many, many doors were opened before us for the future. Daily miracles occurred in Spain as God removed long-standing barriers to the gospel."

Victories in Germany

The years which followed have brought five additional Partnerships in Spain, three more in Germany, and four more Partnerships in France—all at the request of the Baptist leadership in those countries. The news concerning these campaigns spread throughout Europe.

Through one of the contacts given to me by Billy Graham's associate, we met with Peter Snyder of Berlin and were introduced to Gerhard Claas, executive secretary of the German Baptist Union and Joachim Zeiger, home missions secretary in Bad Hamburg.

It was a cold day, and snow was falling as we met in a little restaurant not far from Baptist headquarters. While they ate, I shared with them what had happened in Asia and in Spain and my conviction that God could use anyone, any time, anywhere. Not only could Christian leaders share their faith, but everyone *should* share his faith. I was not sure how the sophisticated Germans would receive such a simple plan, and frankly I was nervous about presenting the program to them. I finished sharing by giving the testimony of our dear friend Woodrow Lawlis, the farmer from Texas who had been such an inspiration to me and whom God had used in such an effective way in Japan. As I finished, Reverend Claas looked up from his plate and said, "If we ever win Germany, it will be through the laymen." He became one of the strongest supporters of Partnership Evangelism from that day on. Later he was elected executive secretary of the Baptist World Alliance and supported and pushed World Evangelism Foundation from that position until Southern Baptists agreed to accept the program in 1980.

Keep in mind that 1973 was a very critical time for Partnership Evangelism. Heated discussion going on among Southern Baptists as to its value and even its dangers. To have the executive secretary of the German Baptist Union come out so strongly for Partnership was a work of the Lord—a major event. In fact, the name Partnership was given to us by German Baptists.

After the 1973 German-U.S. Partnership, Joachim Zeiger said, "We have called this Partnership Evangelism; and it has *not* been partnership in name only; *it has been real partnership.*" It had not been one country telling another "how to do it" but two countries working together in love and cooperation. God granted so many, many victories throughout Germany in that Partnership that an invitation to return was given immediately. It is important to note that Baptist leaders in every country where we had partnership joyously invited us back for at least one and usually more campaigns.

In preaching for Dr. Farris at Forest Meadows Baptist Church in Dallas, I invited all who felt led to participate in the German Partnership to come forward during the invitation. I believe very strongly that *every Christian* who feels the desire to witness can go *anywhere in the world* to share his witness. Not one person need be left out. A young lady, Donella, who had a physical handicap and a speech impediment, came forward saying, "I'd like to be a part of the German Partnership." Because of her speech handicap,

With Joachim Zeiger, coordinator of the U.S.-German partnership

I could hardly understand her, and I wondered if the interpreter could. Nevertheless, she joined the team and went to Germany.

Twenty-five years later, in 1998, as Doris and I were visiting in Germany, one of the German leaders commented again on the testimony of Donella in Mulheim, Germany. We took no better preacher to Germany than Dr. Farris, and we had taken an unusually talented group of team members with us to Mulheim, but Donella's testimony is still the one that stands out in that German community today. God said, "Whosoever will," and He also said, "All things are possible!" He proved it over and over again in Germany and wherever we have given Him the opportunity!

Victories in France

The victories and joys that God gave in Partnership in Spain overflowed from Germany into France. Reverend Andre Thobois, "Mr. Baptist" and pastor of the Avenue du Maine Baptist Church in Paris, invited me to meet with him to share the principles of Partnership. We met in the Intercontinental Hotel in Paris, along with one of our missionaries who had come to interpret. I first

With European Baptist leaders: Gerhard Claas, general secretary, Baptist World Alliance (left); Knud Wumpelman, president, Baptist World Alliance; and Gunter Wieske, director of evangelism, German Baptist Union (right)

gave him a copy of Indy Whitten's book, *The Crusade That Lassoed Spanish Hearts,* and shared the story of Partnership.

At the time of this presentation, Partnership had not yet been accepted by Southern Baptists and the Foreign Mission Board. Thus the missionary, who came with Brother Thobois to interpret, was put in an awkward position. He personally felt that it was out of place for him to be presenting a program that Southern Baptists had not accepted. Later after Southern Baptists officially accepted Partnership, the missionary enthusiastically supported all our efforts in France. Andre Thobois, later joined by Andre Souchon, his associate, presented the idea of Partnership to the French Baptist Union, and French Baptists gave us one of the warmest receptions we as American Christians have ever received overseas. The feature of Partnership that most appealed to them was that it was not an American program; it was a New Testament program, and we were cooperating with them. May we never forget that we are cooperating in Partnership with the host country in the soul-winning program they have found to be most effective. It cannot be done in any other way!

God blessed in an amazing way in France. We had the joy of working in four nationwide Partnerships in France in the 1970s and two in the 1980s. In reporting on these Partnerships in France, I am constantly reminded of the joy and love associated with every partnership!

In one of our Partnerships, Reverend Thobois and Reverend Souchon made arrangements with the mayor's office in Paris for the entire team to be invited to the city hall for a special reception and welcome. No country in the world ever received our teams more joyously and more lovingly than did France.

*With the U.S. ambassador (left) and French Baptist leaders
Andre Souchon and Andre Thobois*

Welcome Banquet in Paris

The U.S. Consul General, Mr. Stone, and U.S. Ambassador and Mrs. Connett joined with us and with Pastor A. Bertrand, president of the Protestant Committee of French Protestants, together with Pastor Albert Nicolas, secretary general of the French Protestant Federation, and several members of Reverend Bertrand's committee in our welcome banquet at the Paris Sheraton. Pastors and laypeople from Texas, California, Oklahoma, Arkansas, Louisiana, South Carolina, Michigan, Missouri, Illinois, Colorado, and Japan joined in one of the most joyous welcome banquets ever! It was the beginning of another victorious Partnership in France.

We teamed up with French churches to cooperate for a week of aggressive evangelism, using the usual translated personal testimonies of each team member and the bilingual New Testament.

One team assigned to a Baptist church in northern France witnessed more than eight professions of faith out of the sixty persons present in their first evening service. One person making a profession of faith was a sixty-five-year-old blind man who lifted his hand and declared to those present that he had not cared enough for God. He said he intended to spend the rest of his life serving Him.

On our World Evangelism Foundation staff was a World War II veteran of service in France, Newman McLarry. When he was barely twenty-one years old, he had been given a battlefield promotion to captain by General George Patton. During the Partnership Newman was given opportunity to address the French Officers' Candidate School, where he shared Christ with those future French officers. As in Newman's case, each team member took advantage of every opportunity to share the message of salvation wherever they went.

The French Partnership Campaign was an encouragement for all involved, and it showed again that people from all walks of life can be effective in sharing Christ across the world. We had team members in their eighties, one who was thirteen years of age, a former television star, and several farmers among the many who went.

A Texas Farmer in Paris

One interesting victory that came out of the French campaign took place in the coffee shop of the Sheraton Montparnasse in Paris. Our teams had just arrived when a farmer from Seagraves, Texas, cornered me in the lobby and said, "Brother Jackson, when are we going to go to work?" I told him, "We have given you this evening off to rest and get over the jet lag. Tomorrow morning we go to work."

He was not satisfied, for he had left his farm and sacrificially come to France to share Christ and did not want to waste any time! In preparation for all Partnerships, each participant's testimony is translated into the language of the country, and up to five hundred copies of this translated testimony printed and given to the team members on arrival. They can then use those testimonies with their bilingual New Testament and witness even when an interpreter is not available.

The next morning this farmer took his translated testimony and went up to the second-floor coffee shop for breakfast. When he entered, he saw an elderly French gentleman having his continental breakfast. He politely laid his testimony on the French gentleman's table and, with a smile, went to his own table to eat and pray.

The farmer watched and prayed as the man would, from time to time, glance at the testimony. Finally the old French gentleman picked up the testimony and read through to the end. As he finished, the farmer noted that the man had a tear in his eye as he took up his pen and at the bottom of the testimony, signed his name saying he was receiving Christ as his Lord and Savior! *No words were spoken.* The moving of the Spirit, the love and boldness of a witness and the Word of God let that elderly French gentleman receive Christ as Lord that morning.

Henry Fonda's Secretary

Dee Briggs was a secretary for Shirley and Henry Fonda, and she had expressed a strong desire to witness in the French Partnership. She would have to raise the money for the campaign and another thousand dollars to pay for two kidney dialysis treatments she would need while in Paris. Without those treatments her life would be in jeopardy. At first her doctor told her she could not leave the United States. But after seeing her determined commitment, our own Colonel E. D. H. Maddox arranged for her to

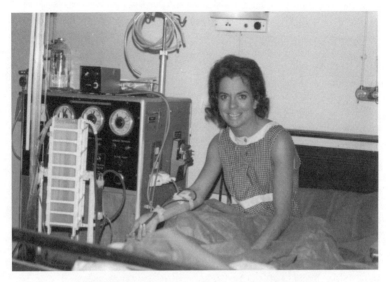

Dee Briggs takes her routine kidney dialysis treatment
while serving as a volunteer in Paris

have her treatments in a Paris hospital, and her doctor finally
agreed to let her go.

Shirley Fonda, without any special interest in the crusades
but because of her love for Dee, loaned her fur coat to Dee and
wished her well. As she left, Miss Briggs said, "I have lived with
kidney disease all my life. Jesus is very real to me, and I want to
share Him with other people." She was an inspiration to all of us
as we saw 450 people make decisions to receive Christ as Lord in
that campaign. Neither health, finances, nor talent can keep us
from witnessing if we have love, concern, compassion, and a
commitment to share His love with our world!

TV Star to France

Tom Lester, television star of the *Green Acres* series, joined our
Partnership to France and generated great interest among many
who ordinarily had little interest in the church. Tom told them,

"I have learned that the greatest thing in the world is to share what Christ has done for me. You can go to church and pray all you like, but if you want Christ to come alive in your life, you must begin to share Him. I think the old quote, 'I witness by my lifestyle,' is a cop-out. Who is going to tell someone about what makes the difference unless we remember that we are the only ones the Lord has to speak for Him. I can go to a church and pray for some old boy to be saved from now until Jesus returns, and he will go straight to hell unless somebody *tells him how* to be saved!"

The story of how Tom got into television was a testimony of how God leads. He said, "When I was asked as a kid what I wanted to be when I grew up, I always said I wanted to be an actor. My friends told me that I would never make it. I was too tall, too skinny, and too ugly, and my Southern accent would hold me back. I graduated from the University of Mississippi with a major in chemistry and biology. I did graduate work to get into medical school. That didn't work out, so I taught school for a while. I loved teaching, but I knew that wasn't what God wanted me to do. One summer I told my parents that I might not make it, but I had to try; and I turned my face toward Hollywood. I was without a job, no place to stay, no friends, and no knowledge of the industry. I even had to follow a map to find Los Angeles." The Los Angeles freeway was the first freeway Lester had ever seen, and when it finally announced, "Hollywood—Next Seven Exits," Lester said, "I took the first one. I wound up on Sunset Strip, made the first right turn and saw a sign that said 'First Baptist Church of Beverly Hills.'

"Through the church, I met another actor, rented a room, and started looking for a job. I got down to only forty dollars in the bank. At a Billy Graham meeting one night, I felt impressed to put ten dollars of that little bit in the offering, and I argued with the

Lord about it. You don't live long in Los Angeles on forty dollars. I lost the argument, so I gave the money." Lester is quick to point out that God expects us to trust Him. The next day an actor friend suggested that Lester use his degree in chemistry as leverage for a job in a film laboratory. "That was an answer to prayer."

He took the job in the laboratory and there met Lauren Cuttle, a drama coach, and as a result appeared in three showcase productions at the North Hollywood Playhouse. He met Lynda Kay Henningan in those showcases and through her father—who created, wrote, and produced *The Beverly Hillbillies*—was asked to read for the part of Eb in *Green Acres*. The producer then gave him a screen test with Eddie Albert, the star of the show, on the following Monday. "On Thursday they told me I had the job. The next Monday I went to work.

"I still marvel about it," he said. "I had no experience at all, unless you count playing the part of a ghost in my high school senior play. There were thirteen or fourteen thousand actors in Hollywood out of work, not making a thousand dollars a year. There were little theater groups all over town with everybody trying to get into pictures. Yet in a city of nine million people, and my not knowing anyone, I wound up in a film that would put me in front of forty million people. Over four hundred actors had read for the part and all were better than me; nevertheless, I got the part. I *know* God was directing my life!"

Victories in England

An Amazing and Miraculous Match!

One of the joyous Partnerships coordinated by the World Evangelism Foundation took place in England in the 1970s. As is true for every campaign, in assigning the team members, we take all the information we can get from the inviting churches overseas and do our very best to assign to each church the kind of people they have requested. We realize that it is not our wisdom in making the assignments but God's leading that makes the difference.

Never was that more true than in an assignment we made for a team going into England. I was not aware that one of our team members, a young lady, was a "little person," when we made the assignments. On arrival in England, and as the American team met their English church and partner, we learned that the home she was assigned to be in was also the home of "a little person" they had been praying for! As our young "little person" stayed in that English home, she shared what Christ meant to her and saw her English partner pray to receive the Lord! Only God can make that kind of assignment.

Later, Arthur Thompson, secretary of evangelism for London Baptist Association, wrote, "We have tried everything, and World Evangelism foundation is the best approach we have ever encountered! Partnership is the most effective plan of evangelism we know in England."

Victories in Italy

Through the years Pastor Andre Thobois and Pastor Angelo Chiarelli had been friends. After the victorious Partnerships in France and after many private conversations, the Italian pastor came to believe that Partnership should be considered for Italy.

At the request of Pastor Chiarelli, and in cooperation with Pastor Thobois and Brother Souchon, Doris and I traveled to Italy to meet with the executive committee of the Italian Baptist Convention. It soon became apparent that Italian Baptists could see no value in a Partnership with American Christians. There also seemed to be some kind of conflict between the Foreign

Mission Board and the convention of Italy. Many objections to a Partnership were raised. After much discussion and no progress, Pastor Thobois and Pastor Souchon stood and shared for almost one hour with the Italian Baptist executive committee concerning the victories God had given in France. After their presentation, Italian Baptists said that any church that would like to cooperate would be free to do so. They would not give their official endorsement, but they opened the door for a joyous and victorious Partnership. Another miracle!

Missionaries Stanley Crabb, Bob Holifield, Dub Ruchti, Ben Lawton, and Mary Lou Moore gave their strong support and love in preparation, and Angelo Chiarelli agreed to coordinate the campaign. To have an effective, victorious Partnership, a *national must coordinate the campaign,* and Angelo did a good job. What a blessed experience!

At the close of the campaign, Angelo Chiarelli commented that "in the beginning, so many of our people said, 'How can we be helped by Americans who have so many problems of their own that they are not able to solve?'" Nevertheless, fifteen Italian churches joined together with the motto: "Jesus saves, liberates, and lets the individual become involved!" Reverend Chiarelli said, "In this campaign, we learned that the *church is not dead! We can* do something! In the smallest church participating, there were seventy-one decisions, and we must keep in mind that there had been only sixty-two baptisms in all of Italy during the previous year. The *gospel can work today,* and that is the good news for Italy *now!*" I do not know of any country where we have gone in which we have felt any stronger the presence of God than in Italy!

Mr. and Mrs. C. O. Sutton, of Amarillo, Texas, were a part of a team that traveled from Rome to Siracusa on the island of Sicily. They were met at the train station by a nervous local pastor and several frightened church members. Nevertheless, as the team pulled into the train station, the pastor, not being able to speak English, held up a sign that read, "I am the pastor. We are very small and very cold. Welcome!" I am sure that this message was intended to convey a warm welcome, but it really described their fears of the situation. The pastor was almost trembling with fear, but as is usually true, after the team and members had worked together for a few days, all became confident and positive in their witness and fellowship. Jim Reid, another team member from Amarillo, said that by Tuesday evening the pastor's boldness and joy were overflowing. He was actually stopping cars in the middle of the street and joyfully handing out tracts and announcements through the windows of the cars! The Lord had taken command of the meeting.

On Wednesday evening, C. O. Sutton, a lawyer, gave his testimony. He had not often given a public testimony. As he read his testimony, Pastor Rapisado interpreted. The interpreter was a pastor from a neighboring village and had been much opposed to Partnership and did not request a team for his church. But because of the need for interpreters, he had agreed to help. About halfway through the American's testimony, the interpreter turned and, with both arms, grabbed Mr. Sutton and hugged him, weeping, and thanked God for bringing him to Italy. God had used a layman, giving one of his first testimonies, to cause this interpreter and pastor to have a complete change of heart about evangelism and Partnership. It was the beginning of revival in Siracusa. People were saved and the church renewed and set on fire.

The big news came the next year when Italian Baptists voted to have a nationwide Partnership and elected Pastor Rapisado, the former reluctant interpreter, to serve as the coordinator for this nationwide effort. What tremendous miracles God continues to give when His people look to Him in faith and trust!

We held this victory celebration at the Cavalieri Hilton ballroom in Rome. It was one of the most inspirational victory banquets ever given by World Evangelism Foundation. At the victory banquets, we try to give at least one team member from each team an opportunity to tell what their team saw God do that week. We do our best to limit each testimony to three minutes, but I have seldom been in a victory celebration that closed much before midnight.

One testimony came from a young man from Odessa, Texas, who had witnessed from his wheelchair all week. When he had heard Jim Humphries, one of our staff members, present the challenge back in Texas, he had thought to himself, *Wouldn't it be great if I could be a part of something like that?* Satan immediately said to him, "You could not possibly go. You are crippled." He prayed and began to wonder, *Why not?* As the invitation was given, he had his wheelchair pushed forward to make his commitment to go to Italy for the crusade! Also amazing was the decision of the boy who had pushed his chair. He too made a decision to go and push his friend in the wheelchair. God blessed, and we heard how God used them all across Italy! There is a place for all in world witnessing!

Bob and Flo Holifield, missionaries to Italy, said, "We had just about come to the place in our ministry here in Italy, where we were considering the possibility of resigning and returning to America to find a more effective place of service. However, because of the victories we have seen here this week, we have come to realize that God is still able to work in Italy, and He can still use us here. We recommit ourselves to Christ and to our missionary task before Him and before you in this service tonight."

Not anyone present failed to recognize the significance of Bob's testimony. Bob and Flo Holifield went on to serve as leaders in the Italian Baptist mission and convention for many more years until they retired. Bob spent his last years as administrator for Southern Baptist missionaries in Italy.

Stanley and Patsy Crabb were very talented and able missionaries of our board and served in Italy for over twenty years. After the Partnership Stanley said, "Words are insufficient to express the appreciation we feel for the way all of you have helped us accomplish in evangelism what needed to be accomplished this past week. The results of this effort have been amazing to all of us!"

Angelo Chiarelli, at the close of the victory celebration, said, "In the name of Italian Baptists, I say thank you for the great help you have given. Our churches now have new life and new hope. We understand once more that the news of Jesus, the Savior and Lord, is the only good news for Italians today."

In the more than one hundred nationwide Partnership campaigns in the fifty countries where the Lord has let us serve, we did not experience anything other than victory in every campaign. The victories were manifested in many ways, but always the victory was clearly understood and greatly appreciated by all present.

Victories in Norway and Sweden

In 1998 as we prepared for the Norway and Sweden Partnership campaigns, we were behind in enlisting the American churches and team members—as usual. We had requests for twelve teams for Norway and twenty-one for Sweden. We had only six weeks before departure. One morning as I was exercising on the treadmill, I prayed, "Lord, I've done everything I know to do. We have made every call that we know to make and written every prospect we know of, but we still lack twelve teams for Sweden and six teams for Norway. If we have the team members to meet the requests of these people, it will be *only because of the miraculous moving* of Your Spirit! We have done all that we can do."

I turned this over to the Lord, knowing that I was asking for the impossible! In my prayer I had also prayed, "Lord, You know of our financial needs, and I ask You to meet them according to Your will." I am sure I did not spend more than thirty seconds praying about our personal financial needs, although they were many.

I turned off my treadmill, went downstairs, and sat down at my desk to cool off and to open my computer in preparation for the morning's work. The first E-mail was from John Floyd, the Foreign Mission Board's director for Western Europe and the one who had invited Doris and me to coordinate the campaigns for Western Europe. Dr. Floyd's message said, "You'll be glad to know that in our prayer yesterday, we were impressed to ask the treasurer to write a check to you for ten thousand dollars to help on the expenses we know you are having." I was bowled over! Yes, we needed the ten thousand dollars. And yes, it was a great help. But my greatest surprise was how quickly the Lord had answered the prayer for help just five minutes earlier! It does not always happen this way, but God always answers our every prayer!

From the moment of our prayer that morning, both telephone lines started ringing so frequently with people volunteering that we could hardly make our outgoing calls! Six weeks later we arrived with every team for Norway and Sweden! God had given one hundred and twenty team members for Sweden and more than seventy team members for Norway. Victory through Christ came in answer to prayer, just asking for victory in His name! "Ask, and ye shall receive."

How God Answered

Shortly after that earnest prayer for the teams, the morning mail brought a letter from Pastor John Shaul, saying, "I received your letter of invitation to the campaign in Sweden and I must let you know that we are just not financially able to go. We must turn down the invitation this time." Not always do I respond in this way, but I felt impressed to call him back immediately. I said, "Brother Shaul, there are many disadvantages of being old, but one of the advantages is that I rarely speak to anyone who is older than I am, so may I take advantage of my age to preach you a ten-second sermon? I received your letter today, and you did not give me a real reason for not going to Sweden. I believe you and I both know that if God leads us to go somewhere, He is able to take care of every need. Would you pray one more day and ask the Lord just one question: 'Lord, do You want me to participate in this campaign in Sweden?'" Brother Shaul said, "You are exactly right! I will pray and seek the Lord's face in this matter one more time." The next day the telephone rang, and Brother Shaul said, "I don't know how, but I believe the Lord would have me do this." Shortly after that phone call, I received a letter from him with a $300 deposit check and a note that just said, "Here goes nothing!" I was so thrilled to know that he was making his decision on faith, believing that he should go. He was the pastor of a key church in a large city, a graduate of two of our best seminaries, and a leader in his city.

A few days later another letter came from Pastor Shaul saying, "I just had a call from my brother who works for TWA, and he told me I will be able to get an air ticket round trip to Stockholm for $250. My wife and I are both going!" From that moment on, God continued to speak and increase his faith and ours. John Shaul found himself in Stockholm with the other 120 team members, rejoicing. He and his wife led a team from their church and took a major part in the Partnership. It was a special joy to kneel in prayer in the ballroom of the Stockholm Sheraton with the 120 American Christians that God had miraculously brought. We thanked Him for the victories He had given and the victories He was going to give! All knelt in prayer as our friend and soloist, John McDuff, sang what was most on our minds and hearts, "Unworthy!" We were inspired and ready—if not worthy—for service!

Miraculous Victory Again

After my prayer on the treadmill, I received a call from my dear friend T. H. Harding of Ballenger, Texas. He said, "After receiving your letter asking us to pray as you searched for team members, I was very burdened and prayed earnestly about it. In fact, on my three-hour drive to Dallas for a committee meeting this past week, I spent most of the time in prayer for the campaign. When I arrived in Dallas, I met a friend of mine, Richard Donovan, and shared with him the burden I had concerning the need for teams for Norway and Sweden. Dr. Harding said that when he told him he had received this urgent request in a letter from Dub Jackson, Dr. Donovan said, 'Dub Jackson! I've been thinking about him all this past week! I haven't heard from him in years. Do you have his address?'" As a result of that call and "chance" meeting, Dr. Donovan, his wife and daughter, together with a team he had enlisted on short notice, knelt with us there in that ballroom in Stockholm, thanking the Lord for the victory of letting us have a part in sharing Christ around the world. *God hears and answers prayer.* "Ask and ye shall receive!"

More Answers

That special morning, walking on my treadmill, looking out across the lake in Abilene, and asking the Lord for help in enlisting team members, was a time when we were deeply aware of God's presence. I have always believed that when God is present, we can take whatever result He may give. Again after that prayer that morning, I received a call from Lester Orwig, a minister in Talala, Oklahoma. He called to tell us that he would be unable to participate in a campaign scheduled for France the following year. I said to him, "I am embarrassed to ask you this because the time for the campaign that is most urgent before us today is only six weeks away!" Nevertheless I told him of the urgent need we had in Norway and Sweden. Lester spoke up excitedly and said, "Norway! When I was in the Air Force, I was stationed at the Oslo airport! It was there that I received Christ as Lord and my call to preach! I have always wanted to be a part of a preaching campaign in Norway. I will do my best to go and lead a team!" He worked hard, made many calls, wrote many letters. Six weeks later, he and his wife had gathered our largest team—twelve persons. We had assigned him to lead the largest Baptist church in Norway in their Partnership. What a blessing! When *God* makes the arrangements, it is an inspiration just to watch!

Victories in Korea

The Korean Partnership of 1975 was one of the largest and most effective Partnerships since the 1963 New Life Movement in Japan. More than eighty-six Baptist churches in Korea received teams from eighty-six American churches. In order to help make interpreters available for all of the teams and to permit missionaries to help, we divided the campaign into two groups of forty-three churches each. The second group of churches arrived in Korea the week that the first group returned to the States.

God Uses a Farmer

One of the teams was assigned to serve in the church where our dear friend Oscar Bozeman served as a missionary. One evening an American farmer stood and shared his testimony in a joyous and positive way. God was clearly speaking through him, but his interpreter, a young seminary student, was a little frightened and hesitant in his interpretation. After one or two exchanges, a gardener, a man hired by Oscar Bozeman to trim the hedges on the mission compound, came forward and told the interpreter, "Sit down, I will interpret for this brother!" Oscar tried to stop him because he knew that he didn't understand English. The gardener replied, "I don't need English. I know what that man is saying!" He took his place as interpreter next to the farmer and enthusiastically began to "interpret" for the Texas farmer by telling what Christ meant to him. When the farmer paused, the Korean gardener would take up the message and in a matching joyful voice, sharing what Christ meant to him and what the Lord was doing in his life.

To this day, neither the gardener nor the Texas farmer ever knew what the other had said, because they were speaking in two different languages. The result of that service was a testimony to all of us. When they sat down and the invitation was given, eight Koreans came forward to say, "I would like to know Christ as Savior." "Not by might nor by power, but by my Spirit, saith the Lord." God gives the increase. True victory does not come from our ability, talent, or experience but by God's Word, His power, and His work! He is ready to use anyone who is ready and willing to be used!

When I shared this story again in Korea recently, the Korean Baptist Convention's general secretary spoke up and said, "I remember that night well—it happened in my church!"

Three Hours from Now

On one beautiful Sunday morning in Dallas, Texas, Doris and I drove to First Baptist Church with very heavy hearts! We were only three days from departure for the Korea Partnership, and the American church that had agreed to take the largest team to cooperate with Korea's largest church had just cancelled! They were scheduled to work in the Yoido Baptist Church, one of the largest and most effective Baptist churches to be found anywhere in all the world. This morning, just three days before departure, we were without a team for this great church.

The Yoido Baptist Church had spent almost a year in preparation and had over one hundred people prepared to work in personal soul winning with the American team. I had called Mrs. Criswell that morning and asked her to present this urgent need to her class of about five hundred members. She had said, "Let's share the announcement together." As we drove on to the church, I was thinking, *It is unreasonable to think we can find a team on such short notice.* Although I normally do not lead a team and also coordinate the campaign, I thought, *I will lead this team myself.* At least that would let the Koreans know that we have a real love for them and a commitment to the Partnership we have been planning for so long. As we neared the church, I was thinking about just what I would say when I realized that I had no message that would fit that situation. Every message I have implies that God is able to do all things anywhere, anytime, and under any and all circumstances. I thought, *If that be true, why am I going to Korea without a team? If God is able to do all things, where is the team?*

I was devastated by the time I came into Mrs. Criswell's class. Immediately she said, "Dub, take just a few minutes and share this special need today." I was embarrassed, as president and coordinator of an organization responsible for a major evangelistic campaign that was to begin in just a matter of hours, to tell these fine people that we had no team to share with our strongest and largest Korean church. To have to make such an unreasonable request before a group of clear-thinking people was very difficult. I told them that the American church had just cancelled and that we had to have at least twelve people to volunteer to take their place and we only had three days before departure! As unreasonable as that might seem, I also had to tell them that the airline had to have their names and passport numbers by 3:00 that afternoon in order to get the special tickets! Peter's walking on the water seemed to me to be far more reasonable than finding twelve people to leave for Korea in three hours!

As I started back to my seat, a dedicated Christian businessman and noted speaker, Zig Ziglar, tugged at my coat and said, "I'd like to pay the way of one person." The victory was starting. Mrs. Criswell called the class to prayer on their knees. One man crawled over to me on his knees and said, "I'd like to go, and I'll pay the way of one more." Now three, and only ten minutes had elapsed. I was encouraged. As the Sunday School class ended and we started to dismiss, Mr. Williamson, a housing contractor, stood and said, "Just a minute, Mrs. Criswell. Dub has tossed the ball into our court. Now what are we going to do with it? I move that we do something now." In the class that morning was Don Carter, owner of the Dallas Mavericks professional basketball team and a dedicated Christian. He immediately passed a note saying, "I will pay half the way for eight people who may volunteer!" Unbelievable, but it was in keeping with God's promises. When the class was dismissed to go into the auditorium for the morning worship service, over $23,800 had been committed to help assure the success of that strategic campaign in Korea. By 3:00 that afternoon, seventeen people had handed me their names and passport numbers to give to the airline. They were able to board the plane on Tuesday for a victorious Partnership campaign, saying again to the world, *God is able to do all things, anytime, anywhere, under any and all circumstances.*

Victories Around the World

Partnership Evangelism Welcomed in All Asia

After effective and victorious Partnership campaigns in many Asian countries, the evangelism and convention leaders of those countries met in Hong Kong January 19 and 20, 1978, to invite World Evangelism Foundation to return for more nationwide Partnerships and to encourage entrance into the countries not yet entered. David Wong, president of the Baptist World Alliance, presided, and those present were Shuichi Matsumura, Japan Baptist Convention; T. S. Shyr, Chinese Baptist Convention; Stephen Noh, Korea Baptist Convention; Daniel Cheung, Kowloon City Baptist Church, Hong Kong; Willie Wickramasinghe, president, Sri Lanka Baptist Union; Ishak Iskandar, president of the Indonesian Baptist Convention; Southern Baptist missionaries Oscar Bozeman of Korea and Peyton Moore, just out of Vietnam; as well as Doris and I.

In this meeting, an earnest and urgent appeal was made for World Evangelism Foundation to continue coordinating Partnership campaigns in Asia. A never-to-be-forgotten moment was seeing Ishak Iskandar pacing up and down saying, "Now—now," when it came time to discuss the date for the nationwide Partnership for Indonesia. We always try to allow at least twelve to eighteen months for preparations, and Pastor Iskandar did not fully understand this. He understood only the urgent need in Indonesia. We always set the date as early as we can while allowing time for preparation.

In the one-week pilot project that had taken place earlier in Pastor Iskandar's church, more than a hundred persons made professions of faith. Pastor Iskandar wanted to see and feel that same victory throughout the convention. Pastor Claude Cone from the First Baptist Church in Pampa, Texas, had led that meeting for World Evangelism Foundation and was invited to come back for the nationwide campaign.

Later we understood Pastor Iskandar's urgency. Even though we set the date to go to Indonesia as soon as possible, he passed away before our teams ever reached Indonesia. The campaign took place, and the Lord gave a wonderful victory, but we missed our great Indonesian leader. We were impressed again that we need to respond to invitations from each country as fast as we can. We are not setting the dates for these victories. God is!

Kenya

Some of the most spectacular and joyous victories in all Partnership have taken place in Africa. In 1988, through the testimonies of two hundred Partnership participants, more than seventeen thousand prayed to receive the Lord in Korea and Africa! It was reported by one missionary that in twenty months, 3,549 professed faith in Mombasa, Kenya, and the number of churches grew from four to forty! Arthur Kinyanjui, president of the Kenya Baptist Convention, was so encouraged that he issued

Jimmy and Carol Ann Draper

a standing invitation to World Evangelism Foundation to come "whenever you can!" Korea, the recipient of more team members than any other country in Partnership history, also issued a standing invitation for teams! There were more invitations to World Evangelism Foundation for Partnership than we were able to accept! The day had to come when all of Southern Baptists would have the opportunity to hear and respond to these invitations.

Jimmy Draper, then pastor of First Baptist Church, Euless, Texas, reported, "On one of our visits with missionary Charles Tope, we knocked on a door and were warmly received by a young army officer. We asked him about his faith and learned that he was a joyous Christian. While we talked, his father, who lived in another city, came in and told us that he had been raised and brought up in a Friends, or Quaker, church." Dr. Draper asked him, "Do you just know about the Lord, or do you know Him as Lord and Savior?" He said, "I guess I just know about Him." "We explained the difference, and in a few moments, he prayed aloud and in front of all in the house, to receive Christ in his heart."

Dr. Draper said, "We then learned that he had been the chief of his tribe and that he had served in parliament for fifteen years." President Joma Kenyatta, the first president of Kenya, chose him to go with a group of sixteen to the Soviet Union for six weeks of study and observation of their system of government. They were then sent to the U.S. for six weeks to observe our system, and the result was that Kenya turned toward the West!

God used an obedient witness in a remote part of Africa to change the direction of a whole country! God is able!

Holland

After the Dutch partnership, Evangelism Director Romke Reiling said, "Words cannot express what a blessing the Partnership in Holland has been. Every church participating expressed great joy and experienced great growth." Most churches said, "We are not the same church after Partnership!" Dr. Reiling said, "In my own church we saw 117 people come to Christ! We are so grateful and plan to keep on cooperating. I believe this is the way God meant for us to work together to win a world!"

Sri Lanka

Willie Wickramasinghe, president of the Baptist Union, reported, "The team of dedicated Christians from the United States went about bearing testimony to their experience of Christ as Savior and challenged our people to turn to Him in repentance and faith. I was greatly impressed with the methodology of Partnership Missions. It was simple and straightforward and carried out in a loving spirit of deep concern for the salvation of our people. They did not try to impose on us their methods. Partnership Missions not only showed us the rationale for evangelism but also the strategy. The most effective means of communicating the gospel is through a person-to-person, live encounter."

Richard Gunasekera, vice president of the Baptist Union of Sri Lanka, said, "Never in the history of our country have we witnessed the hand of God working so effectively within so short a time to reach out to those who need the gospel. This is a new beginning for Sri Lanka Baptists."

England

Arthur Thompson, evangelism director of the London Baptist Association, reported, "The largest post-war gathering of London Baptists came at the conclusion of the third England-America Partnership, September 16–30, 1981. More than a thousand people gathered to rejoice in the blessings God had given. There were 1,167 decisions, and many other commitments not reported. Statistics tell only a small part of what happened."

Denmark

Ove Jensen, past president of the Danish Baptist Union, comments, "The experiences we had through the many years of working with Partnership Evangelism convinced me that the 'people to people' approach perfectly fits our Baptist churches in Denmark."

Taiwan

Tommy Evans, an Olympic medal winner, testifies, "I've had many fulfilling moments in my life, such as winning a silver medal in the Olympics, a gold medal in the Pan American Games, two NCAA championships, three National AAU's, three Big Eight championships in wrestling, and coaching the 1968 Olympic wrestling team. However, seeing an eighty-two-year-old Chinese man, whose wife and friends had been praying for him for many years, come forward and accept Jesus Christ as his personal Savior was the most exciting thing that ever happened to me in my entire life! I thank Jesus for using me."

Hong Kong

Daniel Y. K. Cheung of the Hong Kong Baptist Union said, "Partnership was a wonderful thing to see in our country in 1970. As pastor of the Kowloon City Baptist Church, we witnessed the marvelous victories that God gave, and the many who came to Christ."

Indonesia

Evangelism Director Ishak Iskandar explained that "the pilot project was a new experience in the history of our churches. We saw the greatest number of converts ever, in a one-week revival in one church. Truly we can say more than two hundred people made decisions, a first in the history of Baptist churches in Indonesia. We are now asking for a nationwide Partnership campaign for all our churches."

Japan: The Miracle in the Garden

I had just finished one year with the Billy Graham Evangelistic Association as codirector with Mr. Dan Piatt, working on the 1967 Tokyo Crusade, and was resting in the New Otani Hotel, Japan's largest and most modern! My mind began to wander as I looked out over the magnificent ten-acre Japanese garden that surrounded the hotel. It was a spectacular view over the most beautiful Japanese garden in Japan. I began to think about what it would cost to build a new church in the heart of Tokyo in a place like the New Otani Hotel. It would cost thousands of dollars per square foot! It was unreasonable for a church or even a denomination to think of buying property and building a new church in Tokyo.

Two verses kept coming to my mind: "Ask and ye shall receive," and "All things are possible to Him that believeth."

I picked up the phone and called Mr. Ikezawa, financial director of the New Otani. Although he was not a Christian, he had been most helpful during the Billy Graham Crusade. I asked if he could arrange for me to meet the general manager, Kichisaburo Okada, to share an idea which might benefit the hotel.

Over coffee and cake, I shared my vision with them. "Mr. Okada," I said, "you are building one of the world's finest hotels. Doris and I have long wanted to make a spiritual contribution to the people here in Japan. I will be glad to raise $500,000 and give it to the hotel if you will let us build a chapel in your Japanese gardens. We will staff it with the best ministers from America, and you can provide a suite for them to live in. I believe your guests from Western-oriented countries will be grateful for a Christian chapel here."

My faith was weak, and I watched anxiously as Mr. Okada stirred his coffee. After few moments he said, "I like the idea!" I was shocked, for a small plot of land in their garden would have cost several million dollars, and the rent on a suite in their hotel was more than a thousand dollars per day. Mr. Okada refused to consider the $500,000, for he could not allow anyone else to build on the hotel's land. Instead, he offered their beautiful eight-sided glass tea house for use as a chapel in the day time, while they retained use of it for a restaurant in the evenings. It was the most beautiful spot in the highest location in the garden.

Two years later, we had the dedication service and from that day until now, there has been a service every morning from 8:30 to 10:00, with Scripture reading and prayer. Thousands from all over the world have prayed and worshiped our Lord in that beautiful, God-given chapel!

Col. and Mrs. Don Maddox, our former WEF staff members, served more than eleven years as directors, and God used them to present the gospel. Doris and I never planned to serve there, but just to coordinate and select the directors. However after our days coordinating Partnerships with the World Evangelism Foundation, we volunteered, and for three years we shared Christ with everyone who came through the garden. Some of the most joyful spiritual victories we have ever witnessed took place there. We saw more than three hundred businessmen and women pray to receive the Lord, one at a time! God gave and is still giving victories daily as we ask and believe. Although we had no budget and no personnel, God gave a beautiful chapel worth multiplied millions in the most attractive place in all Japan, and a suite for the leader to live in, for over thirty years!

Many hotel staff members have wept for joy as they prayed and received the Lord. I think of Mr. Nakamura, a wealthy land developer who fell on his face in the chapel weeping and praising the Lord after he prayed and invited the Lord into his life. In my mind I can still see him in the afternoon as he knocked on our suite door and presented Doris with a beautiful Hoya crystal vase filled with brilliant yellow tulips, just to say thank you again. I remember a mother who, after praying to receive the Lord, accepted the Bible we always gave, and walked out praising the Lord, holding the Bible in both hands, like the special treasure that it was! I think of another lady who accepted Christ as Lord and left saying, "I always knew there was something like this, but I did not know what it was!" God is able anywhere and anytime His servants will ask believing! "Ye have not because ye ask not!"

THE FOREIGN MISSION BOARD ACCEPTS PARTNERSHIP

BECAUSE OF THE LONG-STANDING STRONG SUPPORT for World Evangelism Foundation and Partnership Evangelism by Baptist World Alliance executive director Gerhard Claas and by Sven Ohm, director of missions for the Swedish Baptist Union, we were invited to attend their executive sessions each year. In 1980 we met with them in Toronto, Canada. As was our custom, we gave a dinner for the many Baptist leaders from around the world. We always took that opportunity to thank them and to announce the coming Partnerships. In the Toronto meeting we had more than ninety Baptist leaders present, and also Charles Bryan and Bill O'Brien of the Foreign Mission Board. That was the first time in eleven years of Partnership that an official representative of the Foreign Mission Board was present for any of our meetings.

After the Baptist World Alliance-World Evangelism Foundation banquet, at Dr. Bryan's invitation, Doris and I met with Charles and Bill to discuss the possibility of Partnership becoming a part of Southern Baptist strategy. This was a bold and meaningful step on the part of Dr. Bryan and the first move on the part of the Foreign Mission Board toward letting the total church become involved in witnessing overseas.

Charles invited me to go to the Foreign Mission Board headquarters in Richmond, Virginia, to meet with the overseas division to present and explain the principles of Partnership. There was a perfect spirit of harmony in that meeting and a 100 percent acceptance of Partnership. All of us wanted to be a part of what the Lord was doing.

The methods used by World Evangelism Foundation in Partnership were approved by the overseas division and the plan to carry out Partnership by the Foreign Mission Board was adopted and underway! Keith Parks, executive director of the Foreign Mission Board, in a board meeting in Richmond in 1981, made it official. What none of us could do, God did in that meeting, and the miracle many of us thought we would never see took place. Partnership was now free to expand as much as the Lord would inspire His people to launch out! No one then or even now could predict just how far this would go. From no Partnership by Southern Baptists in 1964 to more than thirty thousand volunteers in 2001 is already growth that is hard to comprehend. Thank the Lord and those at the Foreign Mission Board willing to accept and expand the ministry of Partnership.

My faith had been too weak to believe that a large denomination like Southern Baptists would be able to consider a new plan like Partnership in such a brief time. We are grateful to our Lord for this meaningful progress in world witnessing.

One of the comments made to World Evangelism Foundation by the overseas division was, "We want to carry out Partnership exactly as you have done it up to this time." That was a compliment and greatly appreciated, but of course we knew there were many phases of the work that could be and should be improved upon when the full forces of Southern Baptists got behind the plan.

On December 8, 1980, the Foreign Mission Board passed the following resolution:

That the Foreign Mission Board affirms its plan to provide opportunities for Southern Baptist churches to participate in Partnership Evangelism as requested by Missions and National Institutions worldwide.

That the Foreign Mission Board expresses appreciation to World Evangelism Foundation for its contribution to Partnership Evangelism and for its decision to cease its operation on December 31, 1981, in support of the Foreign Mission Board's partnership plans.

That the Foreign Mission Board agrees to work cooperatively with World Evangelism during the phase-out period.

It is anticipated that the Foreign Mission Board will gladly assume financial responsibility for partnership evangelism campaigns according to budgets that will be developed through appropriate channels.

Reaction of Baptist Leaders to the Foreign Mission Board's Decision to Do Partnership

Samuel Maddox, former personnel secretary of the Foreign Mission Board, wrote, "Nadine and I are so very happy that your dream of having a great ministry become fully endorsed by the Southern Baptist Foreign Mission Board is coming to pass."

Brooks Wester, pastor of Park Place Baptist Church, Houston, put it this way: "I fully realize the human element in the movement is largely motivated by the throbbing energy of your concerned heart. My constant prayer is that you might continue vigorously in the service of Christ. We pray that Southern Baptists will catch the vision of the worldwide New Life Movement. The vision from the New Life Movement may not be a cloud any larger than a man's hand, but remember, God can send a deluge of spiritual understanding even as He sent a deluge of rain in Elijah's time. Keep up your good work. Be not weary in well doing, for in due season, we shall have a great reaping of the harvest God planted in your heart if we faint not. We express again undying gratitude for your evangelistic support in drawing Japan and the Orient closer to our Christ. Keep your faith up!"

With joy overflowing, after seeing Southern Baptists officially accept Partnership as a tool for overseas evangelism, Charles Bryan proposed to the board that Doris and I be asked to coordinate the program for the Foreign Mission Board in Richmond. I knew there were more able people available to lead our beloved program of Partnership but immediately said yes. But the board, after hearing Dr. Bryan's proposal, decided that they wanted to have someone lead who would be more likely to make it a Southern Baptist Convention program, rather than, as they put it, "a Dub Jackson program." They did ask us to serve as the overseas coordinators for Partnership, but in all of our prayer and searching, we could not see that as God's will.

A few weeks later, and at the invitation of Gerhard Class, executive director of the Baptist World Alliance, we traveled to Puerto Rico, where the BWA executive committee was meeting. As was our custom, we always had a World Evangelism Foundation banquet with our many BWA friends who were also the leaders of Baptist work in the countries where we had Partnership campaigns.

Following the banquet in Puerto Rico, Duke McCall, who had just been elected president of the BWA, called me out and said, "Dub, we do not have a salary to pay you, but would you consider serving as an associate to the president of the BWA and help me try to inject more evangelism in the BWA?" I had just been told by the board that their plan did not include "a Dub Jackson plan," so Doris and I had to think that this was an open door given us from the Lord to keep on being a part of witnessing around the world. We told Dr. McCall that we would do our best.

Dr. McCall then asked me to serve as director of the men's department of BWA, believing that would be the natural place to rally laymen around the world to witness. I think he was right, and we did everything we could to encourage that ministry.

One highlight of our three years with Dr. McCall was our meeting with President Ronald Reagan in the White House. For an ex-World War II fighter pilot and ultrapatriotic citizen, those moments with the president in the Oval Office will never be forgotten.

Doris and I Meeting President Ronald Reagan in the Oval Office

I had read that President Reagan was preparing for a trip to Asia and immediately contacted him through our senators and others friendly to our task to let him know that we were grateful for him and for his leadership. I asked if the president of our BWA, Duke McCall, Doris, and I could have a moment with him before he left for Asia. He agreed, and for fear I would not have time to share all I wanted to say, I typed out my thanks and concerns before going to the White House. The Marine Guard opened the door to the Oval Office, stood at attention, said, "Mr. President, this is Dr. Duke McCall and Dr. and Mrs. W. H. Jackson." My blood pressure hit a peak as we went into the Oval Office. After the greetings I presented my typed notes to him and remember telling him that if he needed a fifty-five-year-old fighter pilot to help in the battle in Grenada, I was volunteering. That was much in the news at that time. I also had some notes on Japan and Korea concerning the need in Japan and the openness of Korea. He was most gracious.

I did not realize President Reagan had so much humor, but he insisted on telling us one of his favorite stories. He said a commissar was talking to the peasant concerning his crops and asked how they were. The farmer replied, "Great, if you stacked the potatoes up, they would reach to the foot of God!" The commissar said, "Be careful now. You know there is no God!" The farmer quickly replied, "That's OK, Mr. Commissar. There are not any potatoes either!"

When he returned from Asia, he wrote me a nice letter saying that the short orientation on the religious situation in Asia had been helpful and that he had found it just as we had said it would be.

We left giving thanks that Christians were welcome into the highest places of government in our country and praying that God would continue to lead and protect us.

Baptist World Leaders Express Joy and Concern

As leadership for Partnership transitioned from World Evangelism Foundation to the Foreign Mission Board, national leaders from around the world expressed their concern that the principles, purposes, and working relationships of Partnership Evangelism not be changed from what had worked so well for them under the leadership of World Evangelism Foundation. Many made specific requests of Southern Baptists at that time. They wanted to retain the personal touch that was important for Partnership, as World Evangelism Foundation ceased operations and the Foreign Mission Board inaugurated their Partnership program. Many expressed their concern.

Per Midteide of Norway wrote, "Had I read a proposal for a Partnership Campaign in a paper, I would never have voted for it and never would have thought it could be carried out. I would have politely refused the offer. Since Partnership was presented to us through a mutual and respected friend, Reverend Knud Wumpelmann, we received the plan and came away rejoicing and thrilled that God had given us the opportunity. We look forward to the future of these campaigns."

Knud Wumpelmann has served as president of the European Baptist Federation, general secretary of the Danish Baptist Union, and president of the Baptist World Alliance. He expressed a concern common among many overseas leaders: "We think the principles and spirit of the World Evangelism Foundation must be preserved. We believe it is important for the Foreign Mission Board to study the methods and principles followed by the World

Evangelism Foundation in past Partnership missions. We should pray that in the Foreign Mission Board there will not be an approach of 'handing down' a program to us but truly a continuation of Partnership. They must respect the authority of the local church!"

He cautioned, "We do not want to become too organized. We do not want a program that is too clever. We want God's people witnessing, genuinely and from their hearts. Furthermore, Partnership Evangelism needs to be carried on directly with the nationals and in cooperation with the missionaries. Never should it be reversed. The discussion of Partnership and how it is to be executed is best carried out when the wives are present. Dr. Jackson having his wife with him at all times was a great help in setting up a proper relationship for Partnership."

Sven Ohm of Sweden cautioned, "We must not lose the spirit of the small organization in carrying out Partnership through the Southern Baptist Convention. We would not be pleased in working with an organization where the decisions were made in the United States and carried to us. We like the approach the World Evangelism Foundation made in talking with us as decisions were made."

Lewis Mistlebrook of the British Baptist Union staff wrote, "There seems to be no problem in an evangelistic program like World Evangelism Foundation. Our concern is that we not have a program that is dictated to us."

In 1981, the Foreign Mission Board of the Southern Baptist Convention added a Department for Volunteers in Mission to meet the requests from countries around the world.

Despite these concerns, Partnership Evangelism has continued to grow through these years. Today Southern Baptists are sending more than 33,000 volunteers overseas each year.

Jerry Rankin, current president of the International Mission Board, indicated in a recent message that 70 percent of the new career missionaries are coming from the ranks of those who have participated in volunteer work such as Partnership.

Let us rejoice in thanksgiving for the victories and joyous fellowship God has given in the past. Let us in joy and great expectation move forward through the open door of world evangelism that God has set before us. May we always remember the words of Philippians 3:14: "Forgetting the past and looking forward to what lies ahead, I press toward the mark for the prize of the high calling of God in Christ Jesus!"

PRINCIPLES OF PARTNERSHIP

PARTNERSHIP EVANGELISM came into being to involve *the total church* in world witnessing. Matthew 28:19–20 was a directive for *every* Christian, not for a select few.

Partnership Evangelism expresses absolute confidence in God to lead each of us in witnessing here or overseas. It results in the salvation of the lost, strengthened faith of the participants, and renewed joy and fellowship of Christians we visit. Through Partnership we have gained absolute confidence that God's people can go into *any land, anytime, anywhere,* and share their faith, knowing that God can and will give a victory.

1. Partnership evangelism is a program for everybody. No one is left out! If, in setting up an evangelism program, we discover that certain people cannot be included, we can be sure the plan is not God's plan.

2. Spiritual maturity is not a must, even though it is desirable. The indispensable need is for people with compassion, concern, commitment, a love for those without Christ, and a knowledge of the New Testament plan of salvation.

3. The purpose of Partnership is to share Christ with the world, not to promote methods.

Chapter 15

4. Going in humility, not as a people going with all the answers, but going as a people who know that Christ has all the answers.

5. Partnership is possible for all, whether adequate resources are visible or not! *God is able! When He says go, you do not need to see how. Just be obedient.*

6. Confidence in God and in His people. Partnership Evangelism is an expression of confidence in God and His people, here in the U.S. and His people overseas. When overseas, He leads us through His dedicated servants there. We make no compromise of our convictions or alter any God-given truth, but we yield to the leadership of the national, His servant in that country. We know God can lead through His chosen leaders here or there.

7. In Partnership, we are concerned about our use of words. We purposely avoid using the word *help*. We also try to avoid using the words *missionary, missions,* or *foreign.* Instead, we use the words *Christians, sharing,* and *working together.*

8. Partnership should always begin at the initiative of the national overseas. The most effective first contact is always made at the request of the national leader. It is most important that we go to a new country *at their invitation.*

American Christians need to understand that many people overseas would just as soon not have a successful program of evangelism if it has to be presented to them by a foreigner! I believe that in my hometown of Abilene, Texas, that fact would also be true. I do not think that we in our own country are yet ready to throw open the doors of hospitality to Koreans or other great Christian groups who are willing to come and help us! The day will come.

9. After the decision to cooperate in a Partnership has been made, it is perfectly all right for us to ask questions or make

suggestions. It is never acceptable for us to dictate to them. Again and again, we have seen an effective Partnership develop as we prayed and worked together seeking His will and His way in the meetings. Prayer and love will pave the way to victory in Partnership. Never dictating.

10. Remember, it takes more faith on the part of the overseas Christian to receive us than it takes for us to go! They must live with the results of a Partnership, which utilizes foreigners who have little or no knowledge of their culture. They have to work there after we leave!

11. Orientation and preparation materials on the overseas country are furnished by the national Baptist conventions overseas, not the sending organization.

12. Housing for American participants should be in the best possible location, convenient not only for the pastors and national leaders, but for government and city officials who may accept our invitation to participate in various aspects of the Partnership. The selected hotel needs to be one where high government officials will be willing to come.

13. We plan partnerships for only one country at a time. We do not want our people to be thinking of two churches or two countries when they go. We want them to be concentrating on just one church and country at a time. We want at least a full year for preparation for the Partnership.

14. We always explain to our national leaders that the purpose of Partnership is to see people come to receive Christ as Lord *now*. We did not plan to do anything during the week of Partnership that will detract from this goal and purpose of inviting folk to receive Christ as Lord now! This may appear to border on dictating, but there is nothing offensive about explaining the

purpose of our working together before the decision is made to enter into a Partnership. How they choose to carry out the soul-winning program is their responsibility.

15. The date for a Partnership is to be selected by the receiving country. We should be in a country for Partnership at the time that is most convenient for them. It is preferable to have a date set eighteen months to two years in advance in order to give plenty of time for preparation.

16. All Partnership participants are urged to give an invitation to every person they witness to. Never pass that opportunity on to the pastor or team leader. They should always invite the one to whom they have witnessed to receive Christ NOW!

17. Budgets. Many times, if not always, it is more cost effective to have a large and adequate budget to carry out the most effective Partnership possible rather than try to prepare a budget to conserve money that might cause us to miss many opportunities. In our first large Partnership in Japan we used $800,000, but the message was shared with the whole country. It would have taken twenty years and many small campaigns to have the same results. We always need to be ready to do whatever it takes! Ultimately, the apparently less expensive efforts will often be more expensive and far less effective.

18. Gifts to individuals overseas. It is only natural that our team members will meet and come to love and want to help the people overseas. Here are some suggestions.

In most cases, it is unwise for us to *directly* help or even invite persons directly to come to the U.S. for study, etc. We are just not qualified to know who is most deserving after only a week of fellowship. We recommend that you contact the national campaign chairman and offer your help *through him.* If he also feels that your gift or the offer of international study should go to that person, he can suggest a good and effective way for help to be given. If, however, he feels that another person would profit more from your offer, you would want to honor his wisdom in your gift.

Every overseas leader we have worked with has had a great concern about retaining the indigenous nature of the national convention and has asked us to exercise restraint in the use of our money. They have all said that their highest need is for our people to boldly invite their people to receive the Lord.

19. Return Partnerships. Cooperating churches can be involved in a reciprocal campaign. The host church becomes the visitor, and the church that went overseas to share in the first crusade becomes the host for the Return Partnership. At a time acceptable to the host church, a Return Partnership is scheduled, and the overseas church, at their own expense, sends their team to share in witness and invite men and women to Christ in our country. It is better for the sending church to support one person to come than for us to subsidize ten to come!

GOD-GIVEN FAMILY

Special Tribute to Doris

DORIS IS THE INSPIRATION and joy of my life, and I will ever be indebted to her and grateful for our five children. They have been a joy, encouragement, and inspiration. Dr. Ramsey Pollard, former president of the Southern Baptist Convention, once said concerning Doris, "She is one of the most poised and beautiful women I have ever known."

She was one of the spiritual leaders and best-loved persons on campus at Hardin-Simmons University, serving as office secretary for the Baptist Student Union and selected for inclusion in *Who's Who Among Students in American Universities and Colleges.* She also served as financial secretary for the University Baptist Church and secretary for her university class. No one on campus was more respected and sought after for counsel and advice than Doris. She was runner-up for summer queen when we met, and I made her queen for a lifetime!

Our first date was spent working in preparation for a Youth for Christ rally at First Baptist Church in Abilene, Texas. It never occurred to either of us that preparing for crusades would be our work for more than fifty-five years.

Chapter 16

Still sweethearts

Through the years of presenting Partnership Evangelism to spiritual leaders in more than fifty countries around the world, Doris was a vital part of every presentation. Her presence made it possible to have the wives of the other Baptist leaders present, and it changed the atmosphere of those meetings completely. Without Doris it would have been impossible to do what needed to be done.

When we resigned from the Foreign Mission Board in order to do Partnership Evangelism, we lost our income, most of our retirement, and the college scholarships for our five children. If ever a wife had reason to show fear or to complain, she had reason. Nevertheless, not even under those conditions was there ever one word of complaint—only encouragement. Doris always demonstrated unusual love, patience, and fearlessness. Without her, neither this work nor the miracles recorded here could have taken place. Anyone can serve when all things are going well, but she was the same under any and all conditions, serving without fear when even the necessities were not in sight and when there seemed to be little hope or promise for the future! All of this service was in joy. She was supportive when the leadership of our convention was saying in a loud voice, "What Dub and Doris are doing is harmful to the work of the Lord around the world!" Never a complaint! I am grateful that she is now able to see and enjoy the cooperation that is given by our denomination.

On three occasions our work demanded that we sell our home in order to have the crusades—*no complaint!* Doris is very special! God never promised that if we would be faithful He would provide a mansion here on earth. However, He has miraculously provided for us a very beautiful home. Mrs. Evelyn Linebery gave $150,000 to one of our Baptist universities to be used in their nursing program, and she asked them to first lend it to us to buy our home. We are forever grateful to the Lord and to all who made that possible.

Wherever we have gone, Christian leaders, both in the United States and overseas, have expressed their appreciation for Doris. I am forever thankful and grateful to the Lord for giving to me such a wonderful partner!

Doris's trust and faith in God is seen in this poem written during World War II. It was her prayer for the Lord to guide and care for the one she knew He had for her, somewhere overseas.

Prayer for a Love to Be

I know there is a special one
Who's known to You—though not to me,
Who, in Your heavenly plan, someday
Will my true love and partner be.

I'm sure he's facing dangers there
In battles in some foreign land,
So please take care of him for me,
Please hold him in your mighty hand.

And bring him home to safety here,
And guide us as we seek Your will
In loving and in serving You
That we may Your plan for us fulfill.

—Doris Shirley

Our Children

As I thank the Lord for Doris, we both thank Him for giving to us five wonderful, healthy, handsome, talented, and beautiful children! William H. III, born May 21, 1948, served many years as a crusade director for one of the associate evangelists in the Billy Graham organization and continues to be a valuable asset in God's work. Bill has been a real joy for us. During his high school years, he earned many honors in sports and in other endeavors and was president of the student body. He received the best actor's award from the faculty of his university. He and his wife Susan are a constant help and encouragement. They have two boys, Chris and Michael, and one daughter, Olivia, now in college.

Shirley Ann, born June 14, 1951, just before our sailing to Japan, is a registered nurse and a marvelous soloist. She has shown us how to face tragedy and come out with the same positive and joyous attitude God had given to her from birth. Shirley is a graduate nurse from Dallas Baptist University, graduating magna cum laude, and is married to Martin Sloan, a greatly appreciated podiatrist in Abilene, Texas. Their thirteen-year-old daughter Ashley is a cheerleader, and Daniel, Stephen, Julia, and Monica are away in college.

Lynda Annette, born October 20, 1952, in Tokyo, Japan, was a cheerleader in Cooper High School and a beauty queen in Baylor for one of the fraternities. She graduated with a degree in speech therapy. She is forever an encourager and is married to Mike Hughes, longtime Abilene businessman and a Christian leader active in local civic affairs. They have three handsome boys, Clark at home, Lee in Texas Tech, and Craft in law school.

David Lloyd, born November 13, 1953, in Tokyo, keeps all the family computers going. He has also faced difficulties that would stop an ordinary person and gone on to stay faithful to our Lord. He is married to Nancy, another missionary kid, who has shown amazing love and faithfulness in difficult circumstances. They homeschool their two daughters, Kristin and Michelle, and remember with love their son Jered, who went to be with the Lord at age twelve after a heart ailment took him after a one-week illness.

*Back, left to right: Bill and David
Front, Juanita, Shirley, and Lynda*

Juanita Karen, born April 22, 1955, in Kyoto, is still a bundle of energy and joy. She graduated from Baylor University with training in speech and drama and has served as a radio announcer in Abilene, Waco, and Dallas, and now in Columbia, South Carolina. She is married to Steve Hayden, an architect and builder of beautiful homes. Jessica, their oldest child, is a student at Clemson University. Stephen and Preston are in high school, and Sandra is a talented thirteen-year-old poetry writer.

All five of our children have participated in our Partnership campaigns, and most of the seventeen grandchildren have also served overseas in these witnessing efforts. We are grateful.

Family Playing and Praying Together

Traveling often in crusade preparation kept me from being pastor to my own children. We set up a family worship plan that was scheduled once each week when I was home. With active teenagers going in every direction, we found it hard to set a time and day that would fit all. All five were involved in sports and in many church and school programs. We let the *children* set the time and day for this family worship, and we purposely did not set it for the same time each week. We wanted our worship to be special and meaningful—not just routine!

Nothing was allowed to interfere with that devotional time. The first sessions were a little stiff and slow. Normally I would begin by sharing some reports on the joys and difficulties we had experienced in the past week while presenting Partnership Evangelism to Southern Baptists. I shared with them the successes and victories together with some of the difficulties and opposition that we met in presenting Partnership. I emphasized that if God had called, He would also care for and protect and give the victory.

Often I mentioned the names of Christian leaders who supported our work. I tried not to criticize any organization or individual that opposed our work. In those early years of Partnership Evangelism, there was constant and open opposition from our denomination, and our children had to deal with this as well.

After Doris and I had shared, we gave the children an opportunity to share anything they had on their hearts. There were sometimes tears, but also much joy, and a lot of laughter in every one of these devotional periods. We always closed in a spirit of victory through faith with the reading of God's Word.

Today we are scattered across the world and can hope for only one or two family devotional periods each year. Even then, we may not have all our family members present, but at Christmas and Thanksgiving we focus on the family worship! Without worship, Thanksgiving or Christmas dinner would be just be another meal!

CONCLUSION

ONE MAJOR BARRIER to victory in our lives and in God's work has been asking for too little. The goals of our churches and mission boards have been directed toward winning only a small segment of the people. We have no right to alter the vision and command of our Lord when He said, "I am not willing that any should perish." Always our goal and desire is to be a part of world revival.

We must examine our personal goals and the goals of our church and denomination to be sure they coincide with God's plan, which includes *all* people *everywhere*. In many cases, if we should reach our goals and accomplish everything we have prayed and planned for, we would accomplish only a fraction of what God has commanded. Our task and opportunity as Christians is to please Him in all that we do and to serve Him in the way He has commanded. Somewhere along the way we have decided to follow a "more practical plan," but we have set aside God's plan for the whole world.

The New Life Movement and Partnership Evangelism grew out of the desire to be a part of God's plan to win a world now! Unreasonable? Yes, but nevertheless it was and is His command! In the early days of mission service, I found it hard to accept what appeared to be Southern Baptists' plan and goal for Tokyo. What was missing? If Southern Baptists had reached all our goals, and if we had been able to appoint every missionary in our most optimistic dreams, we would never have come close to accomplishing what the Lord was asking of us. That fact and burden gave birth to the New Life Movement and to Partnership Evangelism. We came to recognize that *every* Christian had to become involved and had to become involved *now* if we were to win a world. Career missionaries alone could never accomplish God's plan, regardless of how many we might appoint. No denomination, nor even the combined missionary efforts of all evangelical denominations, could ever appoint enough career missionaries to win our world for Christ. Discovering this fact did not discourage us. Rather, it challenged us to look for the plan that would more nearly please our Lord! This led us to understand that God meant for all of us to be directly involved now!

Most of the victories recorded in this book are those that God gave through the efforts of ordinary Christians who accepted the challenge to get involved in worldwide witnessing now. Looking back, it is hard to understand how we could have overlooked such an obvious and simple plan to share our love for our Lord with all whom He came to save! Today we can clearly hear and understand His voice calling for every one of us to become involved in His plan to let all people everywhere know that He can and will save now! That is Partnership Evangelism. This book has been a report on what happens when God's people respond in obedience to His call to share His message with His world.

If you have not had the privilege of personally sharing Christ with people around the world, ask yourself, *Does the Lord want me to go now?* If the answer is yes, God has promised you the resources, the time, and the circumstances. You can go, and He will go with you!

ABOUT THE AUTHOR

Education

Bachelor of Arts, Hardin-Simmons University, 1948
Bachelor of Divinity, Southwestern Baptist Seminary, 1951

Military Service

U.S. Air Force, P–38 fighter pilot, World War II
49th Fighter Group, 5th Air Force
General Douglas MacArthur's Honor Guard
Occupation of Japan 1945–1946

Missionary Service

51 years total
Missionary in Japan, 20 years
Codirector, Japan New Life Movement
Codirector, 1967 Billy Graham Tokyo Crusade
Founder, Tokyo Baptist Church
Founder, Tokyo New Otani Hotel Garden Chapel
Associate Secretary of Evangelism, Japan Baptist Convention

Additional Service

Founder, Makaha Valley Chapel, Hawaii

Assistant to the President, Baptist World Alliance

Assistant to the President, Dallas Baptist University

Assistant to the President, New Orleans Baptist Theological Seminary

Associate Pastor, First Baptist Church, Houston

President, World Evangelism Foundation. Coordinated more than one hundred overseas crusades with more than ten thousand American Christians in fifty countries around the world.

Honors

Doctor of Divinity (D.D.), Hardin-Simmons University

Outstanding Alumni Award, Southwestern Baptist Theological Seminary

Who's Who in American Colleges And Universities

Junior Class Favorite, Hardin-Simmons University

Family

Married Doris Shirley Jackson, 1947

Children

    Bill Jackson and his wife Susan

    Shirley Jackson Sloan and her husband Martin

    Lynda Jackson Hughes and her husband Mike

    David Jackson and his wife Nancy

    Juanita Jackson Hayden and her husband Steve

Present Positions

President, Worldwide Witnessing

Coordinator, International Partnerships, Southern Baptists of Texas Convention

INDEX